HOME IN INDIA

HOME IN INDIA

A Pilgrimage with People and Poverty
in South India

ANDREW MILLS

Foreword by Deenabandhu Manchala

RESOURCE *Publications* · Eugene, Oregon

HOME IN INDIA
A Pilgrimage with People and Poverty in South India

Copyright © 2021 Andrew Mills. All rights reserved. Except for brief quotations in critical publications or reviews, no part of this book may be reproduced in any manner without prior written permission from the publisher. Write: Permissions, Wipf and Stock Publishers, 199 W. 8th Ave., Suite 3, Eugene, OR 97401.

Resource Publications
An Imprint of Wipf and Stock Publishers
199 W. 8th Ave., Suite 3
Eugene, OR 97401

www.wipfandstock.com

PAPERBACK ISBN: 978-1-5326-6601-8
HARDCOVER ISBN: 978-1-5326-6602-5
EBOOK ISBN: 978-1-5326-6603-2

COVER IMAGE: The photo shown on the front cover was taken from the top of the Murugan Temple hill, Palani, Tamil Nadu, India.

04/28/21

To Helen, Skyler, Jeremy, Damaris
Rey Ann, Margaret, Jeff,
Hannah, Taylor, Doug,
Tony, Krystina, Abril, Jerres,
Rosalina, Winnie, Andrea,
Oksana, Christina, Alex,
Holly, Kurt,
Will, Kyle, Connor,
Chris, Gwen,
Garrett, Savannah, Wyatt
Hendrik, Lorene and Arden

Contents

Maps	ix
Permissions	xiii
Foreword by Deenabandhu Manchala	xv
Prologue	xvii

BEGINNING

Introduction	3
Pasumalai	5
Kodaikanal	11
Bangalore	14
Vatalagundu	16

LIFE IN OUR VILLAGE

Living in Kallimandaiyam	25
Brief Thoughts on Hinduism	35
Our 'Clinic'	37
Village Rows	39
Diversions	41
Getting Around	44
Ramesh	48
Radha's Wedding	52
Tharien	55
Carol Weeber	59
Work Camp	64
Baskeran	65
Health Foibles	68

MY WORK

Loan Societies	73
Food Distribution	75
Veriapoor	79
Valasai	84
Navakani	85
Andersonpatti	90
Clinics	95
Busy Days	97
Funding	99

IN CONCLUSION

A Snapshot of a Developing Faith	103
Leaving India	105

EPILOGUE

Raja Rao	111
Keithahn	120
Newbigin	158
Glossary	167
Bibliography	181

Map of South India showing inset for site-area map
(Courtesy of Google Maps)

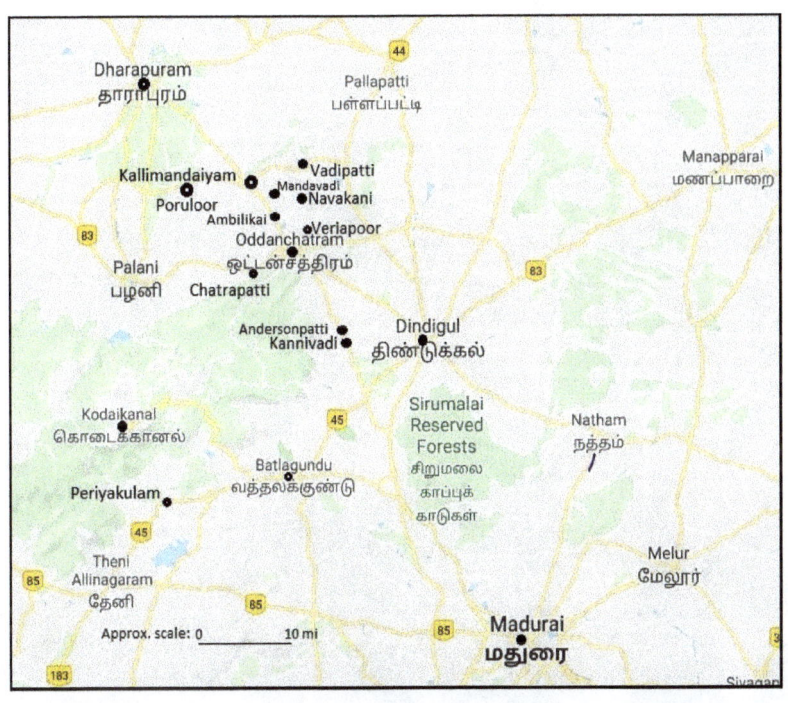

Site-area map showing towns and villages mentioned in book
(Courtesy of Google Maps)

Permissions

The two maps of South India are based on Google Maps of India and, hence, are freely available provided the attribution is included and the conditions stated by Google Maps are adhered to.

All of the photographs displayed in the book are owned by the author, with exception of the photographs of Carol Weeber and Lesslie Newbigin.

Carol Weeber died in 2006 and was never married. Her closest living relatives are her nieces and nephews. I obtained the photo of her by scanning a photo of her on the inside of her book cover.[1] Her namesake niece Carol Weeber Wagner of Beaver Falls, Pennsylvania and her siblings and cousins on the Weeber side have given me permission to use that photo of their Aunt Carol in this book.

Permission to use the photo of Lesslie Newbigin displayed in an IBMR article about him[2] was kindly given to me by Thomas Hastings of the Overseas Ministries Study Center (OMSC) at Princeton Theological Seminary, with the requirement that attribution be given to the 'International Bulletin of Missionary Research' (IBMR), now the International Bulletin of Mission Research, of which Thomas is Editor.

I first tried to reach out to Emmons White's children or grandchildren to get permission to quote translated poems from his book, *The Wisdom of the Tamil People*.[3] The poems I have used are: two couplets from the *Tirukural* given on page 15 and one stanza by the *Shaivite* saint Manicka Vasahar given on page 81 of Emmons's book. Emmons, his wife Ruth, and at least two of their four children have died. I was unable to find contact information from internet searches for his other two children or for the one

---

1. Weeber, *In Lifting Get Under*.
2. Laing, "The International Impact," 19.
3. White, *The Wisdom of the Tamil People*.

grandchild I obtained the name of. Finally, after sending an email message to the publisher of Emmons's book, Munshiram Manoharlal Publishers Pvt. Ltd, in New Delhi, India asking for permission to quote the stanzas, they gave me the desired permission.

Foreword

Partnership is pivotal to Christian self-understanding. It is a conscious moral and spiritual choice that strives to experience the reign of God in relationships of sharing, solidarity and accompaniment, and in those built on trust, respect and mutuality.

Home in India is the testimony of an explorer of such partnership. It is not a mere account of encounters of a traveler to the 'mystic land' of India but one of hope in action, discovering people and their life-worlds, and in the process, one's own self. As the author Andrew Mills confesses: "I gained far more by being in India and interacting with Indians than whatever I may have accomplished in helping the village communities I worked in. India has given me immense rewards derived from Indians sharing their lives with me."

I have not met Andrew Mills, but in his book I encounter a man of strong faith, passionate commitment and profound gratitude as I read through this memoir of his engagement with the people in the Madurai region of Tamil Nadu, India. These resonate with my own theological convictions about God's ongoing mission at the margins of our unjust world, and of the need for the church to find itself at work with God through acts of liberation and transformation. Besides this, the story is all about living out Christian faith in partnership with my people and in my country India, and about the continuing legacy of mission that began with the ABCFM (American Board of Commissioners for Foreign Missions) 200 years ago, continued through the UCBWM (United Church Board for World Ministries) and goes on now through Global Ministries.

It is indeed a privilege for me to write this foreword to this very well-written, engaging and inspiring, first-ever book by the author. I would like to lift four distinct insights on partnership from Mills's reflective sharing. First, one's assertions about inner transformation must be validated through actions that effect transformation out there. Second, a genuine search to find God takes one beyond the familiar and the comfortable, into God's vast and diverse world. Third, is that this account of partnership, of the scientist and a mission worker in Andrew Mills, testifies to the creative possibilities that combinations of positive energies—skills and faith convictions, capacities and calling, and affirmations and actions—can effect. And lastly, Christian engagement in any context needs to be in sync with the biblical witness of God's solidarity with those who are disempowered, those who have been made vulnerable. Andrew walks the reader through the complexity and richness of Indian culture and religion, to learn from those on the underside—the despised and the dehumanized—the Dalits and other rural poor, and their resources, traditions, values and aspirations. The point is that solidarity with the marginalized does not stop with affirmations but makes a conscious attempt to look at the world from a vantage different from those at the center, just the way that God in Jesus Christ does, through the lost, the last and the least.

The Millses returned from India several decades ago. India too has changed much since then. But the story of this memoir remains as a ferment of change, inspiring people to direct their energies and capacities to find meaning and purpose of their lives, not just in the inner recesses of their hearts but in the crucible of experience and in partnership with God's people. As such, *Home in India* offers itself as a resource, a source of inspiration for change, for change seekers and for change makers.

The Global Ministries, the common diaconal instrument of the United Church of Christ and the Disciples of Christ (Christian Church) in the USA, celebrates Andrew Mills's partnership in mission and is grateful to him for this inspiring account of self-discovery while in mission with God's people in India.

DEENABANDHU MANCHALA
Area Executive, Southern Asia, Global Ministries
Cleveland, Ohio
February 6, 2021

Prologue

I started writing this book in June 2020 when we were just starting to take the Covid-19 pandemic seriously. I didn't write it because the virus insisted that I not go out and so had time on my hands. Being retired, I had plenty of time on my hands anyway. My paper to the journal *Groundwater* had already been accepted and was ready to be published in the September-October issue. Also, gone was any work that could bring in some income, as I had been unceremoniously laid off from my job as a part-time computer programmer a year earlier.

No, I wrote the book because one of my granddaughters, Hannah Jordan Mills, urged me to write it. One day, she and I were talking, and she kept asking various questions about my work in India. I realized it was all too complicated to lay out for her understandable answers in any reasonable period of time. One question just led to another question, and another.

Between my wife Helen and me, we have six children and their spouses and 18 grandchildren. I thought at least a few of them might be interested/intrigued(?) to learn what their Dad/Grandfather, or Step Dad/Step Grandfather, actually did and felt during those long-gone days he spent in India. My four children (Hendrik, Skyler, Jeremy, and Damaris) remember quite a bit about India, but they may be short on knowledge about what I actually did there and what things I learned while we were living there.

I never wrote a book before this, unless you count a small self-published volume I pulled together in 2018—*Letters to the Editor: One Voice in the Wilderness*. It consisted of op-eds and letters to the editor I had written since 2006 to local newspapers on issues of peace and justice. I have also published a few articles in scientific/engineering journals.

I have spent a number of years attending schools and colleges. So many that when I started to describe all those years of study to my wife Helen when we first met, all she could say was: "Did you *ever* work?"! Aside from being a perpetual student and my two terms in India (1956–61 and 1967–71) as a missionary, my career has been in groundwater hydrology; I worked for a few engineering consulting firms in succession. I investigated the groundwater flow and the migration of potential contaminants in groundwater for them at many sites in the eastern United States. Also, from November 1980 through February 1982, I was stationed in Egypt by my then employer, Dames & Moore. I served as the water-resources specialist on a team assigned by the Egyptian Ministry of Development to study, and report on, the Sinai Peninsula's development potential.

In terms of voluntary work, in March 1965, I helped organize a busload of 27 of us residents of Davis, California to travel to Montgomery, Alabama, where we participated in the last day of the Selma to Montgomery march. I've also been active over the years with Witness for Peace (WFP) to try and limit the degree to which my country can impose its will on the people to our south. WFP sponsors two-week delegations/tours to selected countries in Latin America. In the 1980s, they operated by accompanying and supporting the people of Nicaragua fearful of becoming victims of Contra atrocities. Today they support the pleas of the poor in several Latin American autocratic countries whose policies are designed to keep the poor down and commit human rights abuses against them when they try to rise up.

This book isn't an autobiography. It's a memoir covering my introduction to India and my meeting and working with Indians during my first term (1956–61) as a lay agricultural missionary to the Madurai-Ramnad Diocese of the Church of South India (CSI). I fell in love with India and Indians. The book covers my feelings being there, some things I learned, the work I did, and, most importantly, the people low and high I met who fascinated me and inspired me.

I was fortunate to have several letters I wrote to my parents and other relatives during those five years. These helped to jar my memory and fill in some details about many of the events I experienced.

Three people I met and worked with were particularly significant to me and my understanding of village India and its needs—Raja Rao, my Tamil teacher, and two missionary colleagues, Rev. Ralph Richard Keithahn and Bishop Lesslie Newbigin. I decided to put their stories and their interaction with me in the Epilogue to set them apart uniquely.

I realize looking back on those days in India modern eyes might rightly see marked elements of paternalism. The very way missions in India operated earlier usually went hand-in-glove with the British colonial masters. But when I went out to India, the country had been independent for nine years. And after 1959, all the leadership of my CSI Diocese was in the hands of Indians, and we members of the Madurai Mission worked under them.

But there was a clear sense of white-missionary privilege akin to the *white privilege* that we're just now starting to talk about in this country. So we missionaries to India from America, Europe, and Australia as a carryover from the colonial era, even after Independence, were treated with special respect by most Indians. Not only respect, but we were freer to do almost anything we felt was worthy of our time than were Indian church leaders. And of course, our salaries were usually significantly higher than those of our Indian colleagues. Hence, some missionaries strove to live more simply than before to be on a more equal footing with our colleagues.

My family and I moved to the village area where I did most of my work in October 1958, after half of our first five-year stint was almost over. The village where we lived, *Kallimandaiyam*, was located in the Diocese's far northwestern corner, a particularly needy area. Before moving to *Kallimandaiyam*, we were in Bangalore learning Tamil at a language school, and then in Vatalagundu, in another part of the Madurai-Ramnad Diocese, where we continued studying Tamil and where I raised Leghorn chickens so I could distribute fertile eggs to local people.

I was grateful to the American Board of Commissioners for Foreign Missions (ABCFM) for selecting my family and me to send to India in 1956. Raymond Dudley, who was then Secretary for India and Ceylon under the Board, played the primary role in sending us out and was always kind to us, even visiting us in India in early 1957 when we lived in *Vatalagundu*. Raymond was instrumental in the Board's sponsoring us for a year of mission training and Biblical studies at the Hartford Theological Seminary in Hartford, Connecticut, during the school year 1955–56 before sending us to India. The courses we had there on India and mission studies, linguistics, New Testament, and theology were invaluable.

The ABCFM became the United Church Board for World Ministries (UCBWM) when the Congregational churches and the Evangelical and Reformed denomination joined to form the United Church of Christ in 1957. And under the new (in 1958) Secretary for India and Ceylon, Telfer Mook, and his wife, we received excellent guidance and support for the work. His support and the freedom he allowed me, I believe, led to my work being more effective and satisfying.

In 1967 the UCBWM work in Southern Asia, including India and Sri Lanka, functionally merged with that of the Division of Overseas Ministries of the Disciples of Christ. In 1996 the shared foreign ministries of the two denominations officially became 'Global Ministries' under a new board, 'Common Global Ministries Board'.

A note about Dalits: The people I served during my first term in India were the landless *Dalits*; hence, it behooves me to give the reader an introduction regarding this group of people in South Indian society. The word *Dalit* refers to people in India who had previously been known as Outcastes, meaning they were so low on the societal scale that they were considered outside the caste system. Of course, sociologists rightly tell us they were indeed a part of the caste system but had been assigned to the lowest place. The word '*Dalit*' means 'oppressed, crushed, broken, or trampled over', which expresses how these people have been treated by their countrymen over the ages. During the time when I was in India, the term '*Harijan*' was usually used to refer to the *Dalit* people. Gandhi insisted on using that name to refer to the *Dalits*, '*Harijan*' literally meaning 'people of God'. But starting in the 1970s, there has been a growing new identity among the *Dalits* that indicts the wider caste Hindu society for the stigma and suffering *Dalits* have endured through the ages. The meaning of the word *Dalit* clearly emphasizes that indictment and holds the society responsible for their oppression.

Rev. Deenabandhu Manchala, Southern Asia Area Executive for Global Ministries, has written extensively about *Dalits* and their condition in India's caste system[4]. His role in Global Ministries is comparable to Raymond Dudley's and Telfer Mook's roles under the UCBWM during my time in India. Deenabandhu has pointed out that even within the churches, Christian *Dalits* suffer similar segregation, oppression and discrimination, and the same social, educational, and economic disabilities, but now at the hands of their fellow Christians of the upper castes. He notes that conversion into the new faith doesn't seem to have redeemed Christian *Dalits* from their 'dalitness' or the stigma of 'Untouchability'. The *Dalits* constitute approximately 80 percent of all Christians in India.

I am grateful to the Diocese of Madurai-Ramnad of the CSI, the late Bishops Lesslie Newbigin and George Devadass, and all the pastors I interacted with for their strong cooperation, guidance, and kindness in their interaction with me and the work I did. I'm equally grateful to the late Rev. Packianathan, pastor of the Oddanchatram pastorate, with over 50 village congregations.

I owe my family including my parents strong thanks for all the ways they helped me in India. I acknowledge that in this book I have given short

---

4. See for example, "Taking the bull by the horns," in *People's Reporter—A Forum of Current Affairs*, Volume 33, Issue 14, July 25-Aug 10, 2020, Mumbai India by Deenabandhu Manchala.

shrift to the lives and feelings of my closest family members. I made the decision to limit this memoir to the story of my own experiences and thoughts in India during 1956–61. But in the background to the story of this book are Jane (my ex-wife) and my oldest son Hendrik both of whom accompanied me to India, and my second and third sons, Skyler and Jeremy, who were both born in India during that first term. Our adopted daughter Damaris was not yet born in the years covered in this book. I owe a debt of gratitude to each of them for supporting me in many ways during the first term.

As so many have said about their own experiences overseas, I gained far more by being in India and interacting with Indians than whatever I may have accomplished in the village communities where I worked. India has given me immense rewards derived from the Indian people's sharing their lives with me.

I'm grateful to my wife Helen for her thorough reading of the early draft and for suggesting needed corrections. I also wish to thank my friends from India days who were kind enough to read the early draft of the book and offer comments and suggestions—Patricia Gass and Ruth Lockwood.

I owe Dr. Mearl Marie Keithahn, Dick Keithahn's older daughter, a debt of gratitude for providing me detailed information about her father's life that I didn't know before. I particularly want to thank the following for their love and unswerving affection toward me and for encouraging me in writing this book: my wife Helen, my children Skyler, Jeremy, and Damaris, and my grandchildren Hannah, Jerres, April, Tony, Taylor, and Rosalina.

Andrew Mills
December 31, 2020
Lower Gwynedd, Pennsylvania

BEGINNING

INTRODUCTION

I'm an idealist and a romantic. That's how I've been for at least the last 80 of my 90 years. I believe that world peace is still possible if we work at it. My eyes filled with tears at the death of Congressman John Lewis. I get goosebumps just listening to the songs of Sound of Music or to 'Somewhere over the Rainbow' by Sarah Vaughn. I've also been fearful most of my life.

Somehow all this is connected to my wanting to protect those whom the world looks down on and often abuses, and improve their lives. For there but for the grace of God go I. And I believed, and still believe, all of us are children of the family of God, and we need to take care of each other. I felt a strong calling to serve the poor of India in his name. I wanted to be on his team.

This was the essential core of my personality and my developing faith that led my ex-wife (Jane) and me to serve in South India as lay agricultural/rural missionaries under the American Board of Commissioners for Foreign Missions ('Board')[1]. We became members of the American Madura Mission (the British had called it 'Madura' instead of the correct name *Madurai*); at the same time, we were workers in the newly formed Church of South India (CSI).

From that first day in March 1956, when Jane, one-year-old Hendrik, and I arrived in Madurai in South India, I just loved being in India. Starting then and ever since, India was the place that felt more like home than any other place on earth[2]. Later I would hear foreign visitors complain about

1. The mission board for the Congregational churches at that time
2. Compare to famed Sherwood Eddy's feelings about working in India as a missionary in the first decade of the 20th century. Eddy in his little book *Supreme Decision*, written with J. R. Mott as it was reissued in 1906 wrote: "Here, in the so-called 'foreign' field, I have 'found' myself; I have come to my own...India is home to me now. I have come to love India," as related in Nutt, *The Whole Gospel for the Whole World*, 73. (My family and I wound up living for a year and half in the very same bungalow in Vatalagundu as he and his family had decades earlier.)

India. But what bothered them didn't bother me at all. It was all part of the differentness I enjoyed. It was wonderfully exciting—so much to learn. I wondered at the many adventures in the villages as yet unknown that lay in front of me. It was as if God had given *me* India as a big present.

To me, India and its people were beautiful, and the way they dealt with the difficulties and frustrations of living was usually an inspiration and taught me something every day I was there.

I came to India because I wanted to help improve the lives of poor people in the rural areas, particularly poor farmers. As it turned out, the farmers weren't the ones who needed the most help; they were practicing subsistence farming in our part of South India quite successfully on their small 2- to 10-acre irrigated plots. The poorest people in the rural areas were the landless Dalits, whom I describe in the Prologue. Most Dalit men would receive a portion of each harvest from the higher-caste farmers for whom they worked, but they usually got significantly less than the farmer kept for himself and his family. So I worked to improve the lives of the Dalits in my area.

PASUMALAI

As our overnight train from Madras (now *Chennai*) neared Madurai and I saw the green rice paddy fields on both sides, I said to myself, "So this is what our new homeland looks like!" I was thrilled. We were met right on the platform in Madurai by very senior missionaries of the America Madura Mission (AMM), Emmons and Ruth White. We had just become the newest members of the AMM. The Whites hosted us in their home in Pasumalai, a suburb of Madurai, for the first two or three days until we were sent up to Kodaikanal ('Kodai') in the 'Palani Hills' to start studying Tamil. The name 'Palani *Hills*' is a misnomer, for they are *mountains*, part of the Western Ghats, which reach an altitude of more than 7,000 feet and extend on India's western side from near Cape Comorin to as far north as Gujarat, north of Bombay.

In 1947, the American Madura Mission was subsumed under the Madurai-Ramnad Diocese of the Church of South India (CSI). That was the year the CSI, a united church, was formed as a new denomination. Five different church traditions were brought together in the CSI: Anglican (Episcopal), Congregational, Dutch Reformed, Presbyterian, and Methodist. All these churches had been established in India through the missionary work of churches in Europe, America, and Australia. Since the creation of the CSI, missionaries under the AMM, for example, didn't work under the mission any longer but under the Madurai-Ramnad Diocese and its officials, including the diocesan bishop Lesslie Newbigin, a missionary under the Church of Scotland.

So how does the Christian community rank in terms of numbers in India? The percentage of Christians (Catholic, Orthodox and Protestant) nationwide was about 2.3 percent in those years, and hasn't changed very much since. Hindus made up about 84 percent in those days and Muslims about 10 percent of the population. Fifty years later, the percentage of Hindus was about 80 percent and Muslims made up 14 percent.

The Whites lived in a very large house, called a 'mission bungalow' with a spacious veranda all around. The house was in a large mission compound containing several CSI schools and three such bungalows, each bungalow occupied by one missionary family. Ruth really took to one-year-old Hendrik and announced that she and Emmons would be Hendrik's grandparents in India, even though she and Emmons were just a year away from retiring to a missionary retirement home in California.

I always looked forward to mealtime during those first few days with the Whites. Everything was delicious as prepared by their Tamilian cook, even though the dishes were mostly Western-style. Breakfast was particularly interesting when we had porridge. The first time their cook served us porridge, it looked like chocolate pudding. I said to myself, "How funny that they would serve chocolate pudding for breakfast!" But it was not chocolate pudding, but a particular kind of millet, *ragi*. It was served as porridge in the most disagreeable way, even when served with sugar or local syrups. It turned out that many other missionaries in the area would also eat ragi porridge for breakfast, believing that this millet would give them more nutrition than rice-based Indian breakfasts, which was true. I learned that almost any other kind of millet, grown commonly in our area, for example, *kumbu*, *thenai*, or even sorghum, can be served as porridge in a tastier way with equally good nutrition. And there was even an appealing alternative to *ragi* porridge, namely *ragi puttu*, in which the *ragi* in the form of meal is cooked by steaming and is delicious when served with coconut.

Emmons was particularly interested in my learning Tamil and shared with me translations of some of the classical poems in Tamil and instrumental and vocal examples of Carnatic music, the classical music of South India. He had made Carnatic music his main hobby. For many years, he had retained a local Carnatic music guru to teach him the systematic musicology and the art of singing the Carnatic way. Emmons learned the basics of presenting a musical sermon called *kalakshepam*, sung in Carnatic mode by a preacher. In earlier days, *katha kalakshepam* used to be presented by Hindu classical artists to tell stories from Hindu mythology in song. On a few occasions, Emmons presented the stories of Jesus as kalakshepams in church services, instead of regular sermons. Unfortunately, these performances didn't come across as that authentic and were almost embarrassing, so our Tamil teacher Raja Rao later told me. (For more about Raja Rao, see the Epilogue.)

But Emmons achieved more than most missionaries who attempted to become proficient in Carnatic music, and just his dedicated interest in the subject endeared him to many Hindus. Also, he and Ruth both spoke Tamil well. In his retirement, Emmons wrote a short book entitled *The Wisdom of the Tamil People*.[1] He summarized sympathetically the Hindu beliefs of the Tamils, particularly presenting and appreciating the spiritual poetry of the Shaivite and Vaishnavite saints.[2] UNESCO accepted his book in their Indian Series of the Translations Collection.

During our first year, Emmons tried his best to get me to take up Carnatic music, and he recommended his teacher to me. But as it turned out, I was to be stationed in rural areas 30 or more miles from Madurai, and it would have detracted from my work to have to go into Madurai to meet with his teacher on anything like a regular basis. So despite my early appreciation of Carnatic music, I had to decline his offer.

We were grateful that our first introduction to India and the Mission was with the Whites. They were the most congenial hosts we could have had.

Up the hill from the Whites' bungalow was the missionary bungalow where Lloyd and Olive Lorbeer lived. They were a very energetic older couple. Lloyd served as manager for several CSI schools, and Olive was a nurse who had worked in the CSI hospital in Madurai. Lloyd was nothing but enthusiastic, with love for everyone he met. But as a downside, his Tamil pronunciation left something to be desired. He was open at all times to discussions and cooperation with Hindus. Many's the time when he would visit villages by public bus; he'd tie his bike up on the roof of the bus. Then when he got as close as he could to the village where he was headed, he would have the bus stop, and he'd take his bike down. Then he would cycle the rest of the way, much to the pleasure of people he met along the way. Olive was perhaps the kindest, most compassionate person I think I've ever met.

Lloyd earnestly believed in Gandhi's concept of 'basic education,' and the Indian government was vigorously promoting that philosophy of education in all its schools. But Lloyd found himself in conflict with Lesslie Newbigin, our bishop of the Madurai-Ramnad Diocese, on common worship that was part and parcel of *basic education*. The bishop insisted that no CSI school in his Diocese should practice compulsory common worship between Hindus and Christians. Lloyd felt that it was essential to include common worship at the *basic* training school in Vatalagundu, one of the schools he managed for the CSI.

One of Lloyd's reasons was probably that a school would be more assured of continuing government support if it adhered to all the *basic education* tenets. As a result of his disagreements with the Bishop, Lloyd resigned

1. White, *The Wisdom of the Tamil People*.
2. Shaivite saints are worshipers of Shiva and Vaishnavite saints are worshippers of Vishnu, two of the three primary gods in the Hindu pantheon.

from his position as manager of the Vatalagundu training school, and his fellow missionary and mine, Dick Keithahn, replaced him. (For more about Bishop Newbigin and Dick Keithahn, see their chapters in the Epilogue.)

Gandhi's 'basic education' represented a break from the former prevalent system of education. He believed that a child's education should begin with teaching a craft to enable him/her to produce something useful right from the start. He further insisted that teachers should present the subject matter scientifically so that the child will know the why and wherefore of every process.

His *basic education* ideas were rooted in village life, not so much urban life. The idea was that with a practical education, young people would have the training and skills necessary to make a living in their village, and would allow them to play a responsible and valuable role in village life. They wouldn't have to follow the pattern of young people migrating from their villages to the cities.

Back in Pasumalai, just down from the Whites' bungalow in Pasumalai was the bungalow where Charles and Mary Ellen Heineman lived with their four children. Their youngest, Louise, was a few months older than our Hendrik. Charles headed up the Pasumalai Trade School under the CSI located on their large compound. The school offered programs in automobile mechanics, carpentry, and welding, with scholarships to poor, often Dalit, students.

Charles and Mary Ellen came to India separately and unmarried in the 1940s. She came out as a teacher under the Methodist missionary board to what is now the Indian state of Gujarat, north of Bombay. He was a trained engineer and had also received seminary training when joining the AMM under the ABCFM. After Charles and Mary Ellen met and fell in love, she agreed to join him in the AMM, replacing her Gujarati studies with new Tamil studies. When the Millses arrived on the scene in 1956, she and Charles spoke Tamil very well. Both Charles and Mary Ellen were pacifists, so they were comfortable with the concept of *ahimsa*[3], a vital part of the Gandhian philosophy that inspired the push for Indian independence until it finally happened in 1947.

The Heinemans were well known for trying to live simply amid so many poor people in India. Living simply was a goal of a minority of missionaries, its purpose being to be more on an equal footing with their Indian colleagues.

---

3. Respect for all living things and avoidance of violence toward others.

Sometime in 1957–58, the Heinemans would leave the city environment and find their home in more spartan rural living quarters. About two years later, we visited them when they were living in quarters fashioned from a shelter in the weekly market place in Tiruvadanai, Ramnad District, east of Madurai. I don't think we could have done that; it was an uncomfortable way of living. Both Charles and Mary Ellen were wonderful in their care and compassion for the poor in the many ways they responded to requests for help. Mary Ellen was a saint in my mind, comparable to Mother Theresa. And Charles was one of the missionaries in India I admired the most.

I interacted with Charles later in a water-development project. During our second term in India, 1967–71, I was assigned by the UCBWM to the Indian non-profit, Action for Food Production (AFPRO). I worked for the latter as a Water and Soils Specialist. Among other duties, I oversaw some of AFPRO's water development activities, including well drilling and setting up and managing groundwater investigation teams to locate favorable sites to install wells.

There's a popular method to improve the yields of existing large-diameter (15 to 30 feet) irrigation wells sunk in rock. It involved drilling small-diameter holes 10 to 15 feet long from the bottom or the sides of existing wells. Sometimes considerable improvement of the yield resulted, sometimes not. It depended on whether or not the auxiliary holes intercepted a water-filled fracture or set of fractures. To do this, we used a medium-sized air compressor located at ground level connected to an appropriate jackhammer, in-hole steel rods, and hose at the bottom of the well.

Charles Heineman applied to AFPRO for one of these sets. After he received the equipment and set up his Indian crew, they had success in improving yields of many dug irrigation wells in Madurai and Ramnad districts. A couple of times, I went out to see him and his equipment in action. Charles didn't just stand aboveground supervising, but often enough he was down in the well after it was pumped out to allow the operation to proceed. Usually, the only way to get to the bottom of the well was via crude steps cut into the side of the rock well. Charles and his crew members would get down into the well by gingerly making their barefooted way step by step to reach the bottom. I told Charles that I was concerned about their falling, but he was unafraid, and I never heard of any serious accident happening while he led the project.

That was the last time I would see him in India. The next time I saw him and Mary Ellen was quite by accident when they and I were part of the historic anti-nuclear-weapons demonstration in New York City on June 12, 1982. Somehow, suddenly I literally bumped into them amidst the vast throng of an estimated one million demonstrators! They had decided they needed to be at the demonstration so drove to NYC from Tennessee, where they had retired to. My family and I were living in New Jersey then.

I was able to see Charles and Mary Ellen a couple times in 1995 after they had retired to Tennessee, and I was living in Newtown, Pennsylvania. We first met at a reunion of UCBWM missionaries to India held in Pleasant Hill, Tennessee, then a few days later in their apartment in Waverly, Tennessee. Mary Ellen was fully-occupied volunteering part-time at a local recycling center and taking care of Charles who was not well.

KODAIKANAL

Four days after we arrived in Pasumalai, we went by bus to Kodaikanal ('Kodai') to begin our first lessons in Tamil. It was a beautiful ride up the *ghat* road but a little scary, as the road was narrow, there were several hairpin turns, passing other vehicles was breath-taking, and the low walls/railings at the side of the road often seemed skimpy. But we made it, as everybody does, and we settled into the left half of 'Central House,' one of several houses in Kodai owned by the Mission to provide missionaries with beautiful, cool places to vacation during April and May, the hot season. Kodai was at an elevation of about 7,000 feet, and from the famous Coaker's Walk in town you look down onto the little city of Periyakulam on the plains, 6,000 feet below. It's a stunning view. Eucalyptus trees are everywhere, and their scent adds to the beauty of the place—a perfect place to escape the heat of the plains if you have the wherewithal to afford it.

On Monday, we started our Tamil classes with Professor P. Jothimuthu, who headed Tamil Studies at American College in Madurai. American College was one of the many Christian institutions started by the American Madura Mission and was now managed by a college board. Professor Jothimuthu was an example of the many success stories brought about by the Madura Mission. As a very bright lad of Dalit origin, he studied in several mission schools and achieved higher and higher stations in the education world. For several years he had been well known as an expert in translation, translating much of the ancient Tamil Sangam literature into English. The Tamil Sangam comprised the famous Sangam academies of poets and scholars who did most of their work in Madurai during the period from approximately the sixth century BC to the third century AD.

Jothimuthu and his wife had three beautiful daughters. One of them, Padma, had earlier been romantically involved with an American man, David Gallup, who met her when he was an exchange student to American

College from Oberlin College between 1952 and 1955. They married and went back to America, where he began his theological studies for an MDiv degree. Three years later, they came back as a missionary couple in the Madura Mission under the CSI! They were first assigned to Aruppukkotai, about 30 miles south of Madurai.

We were lucky to have Jothimuthu as our teacher to start our Tamil studies. He was patient with us and cheerful all the time. We attended morning classes in Tamil from 9 to 12 and then worked on assignments on our own in the afternoon. I found it exciting to learn such an ancient language with its distinctive script. And based on a beautiful course we had had in linguistics at the Hartford Theological Seminary in 1955, we understood how important it was to get the pronunciation right. There were three of us in Jothimuthu's class: Jane and I and an English missionary lady belonging to the Missouri Synod Lutheran Church mission. Our classes were held in a small building on the Missouri Synod Lutheran compound.

Immediately across the ghat road from the Missouri Lutheran Synod compound was the 'Missionary Union.' Missionaries from several mission boards vacationing in Kodai would gather at the Missionary Union every Wednesday afternoon during the season (April-May). But Indians were not present at these 'teas.' I don't think members could even invite them as guests. As far as I could see, you were a member if you just walked into the building while white. On one occasion at one of the teas, I complained to Mim Brown, a missionary lady in our mission, that I felt uncomfortable coming to these gatherings when it seemed that Indian friends were effectively excluded. She said she saw nothing wrong if missionaries wanted to mingle with other missionaries. Thank God for Padma Gallup as she apparently had magically become 'white' and so could attend the social gatherings at the Union! I attended these gatherings only a few times, unwillingly.

I learned about the Kodaikanal Ashram Fellowship; my missionary colleague Dick Keithahn was its principal manager and leader. The ashram was located about two miles from town, and I remember walking the distance many times. The accommodations were not quite as comfortable as the missionary vacation houses, but they were available on a first-come-first-serve basis to people of all races and religions. The next year we would stay at the ashram rather than in one of the mission houses for our vacation. The ashram had many interesting programs which ranged from hiking to evening group discussions from many perspectives on spiritual and even political topics, and then games. Meals were shared in common, which led to even more enlightening discussions. Every guest was assigned some job for the day, for example, cleaning or meal preparations. Morning meditations were held at the 'Rock of Vision,' a nearby sizeable flat rock directly overlooking the plains 6,000 feet below.

I remember when I alone, or with one of my sons, hiked down the mountain from Kodai to the plains below, a fair distance horizontally and vertically. Some more athletic people even undertook the more strenuous hike of climbing from the plains back *up* to Kodai. I and most others were quite happy just to catch a bus to take us back up. It was invigorating and strenuous enough climbing *down* through jungle. I often hoped I would see a wild elephant during those treks, but never did.

Our second son, Skyler, was born in Kodaikanal two years later, June 12, 1958. About a week or ten days after he was born, we were ready to come back to where we were living on the plains at the time, Vatalagundu. Dick Keithahn, my missionary colleague, was kind enough to offer to bring us down in his old jeep. It was a distance of just 40 miles but a decline in altitude of 6,000 feet. We all piled in the jeep and started off. About three-quarters of the way down the ghat road, we suddenly ran out of gas. Dick always tried to live frugally, but he carried that virtue a little too far that time.

So what we did was for Dick and me to be outside the jeep pushing, while Jane and the two boys, one being one-week-old Skyler, remained inside. It was tough during the short distances when the road ascended rather than descended. Eventually, we got down to the bottom and were able to push the jeep relatively easily on the flat until we reached the first petrol bunk (gas station). Maybe that early experience of being in a jeep while it was being pushed for a couple hours deeply influenced Skyler so that he would always adore cars, as he does. When he was two-plus years old, he insisted on cozying up in his crib to a (clean) spare motorcycle carburetor I had, instead of a teddy bear.

BANGALORE

In June of 1956, we set off with our things to the missionary language school in Bangalore, now known as 'Bengaluru.' It involved taking the bus from Kodai to a rail station called 'Kodai Road,' where we boarded an overnight train to Madras (*Chennai*), and thence a day train from Madras to Bangalore. With ten other missionaries, we moved into a dormitory-like building, which was on the compound of the United Theological Seminary. Each family, couple, or single person had their own bedroom, and we all had to share just five bathrooms. We students ate all our meals in a common dining room. We had common prayers after dinner before we retired, and we all took turns leading the vespers. One of the more evangelical of the students took it upon himself to judge the validity of the person's faith leading the prayers. He announced that Jane lacked the necessary sincerity in believing in Jesus's saving grace one evening after she led the prayers. While when it was my turn, I miraculously passed his scrutinizing test.

The languages taught at the language school included three of the four Dravidian languages—Tamil spoken in the city of Madras (Chennai) and to its south in Madras state (now Tamil Nadu), Telugu spoken in the part of Madras State north of the city of Madras, and Kannada spoken in Bangalore and to its north and west. Our Tamil instructor was Mr. Jeevanasen, actually a brother of Jothimuthu! He was an excellent teacher and quite a funny man; his name means 'lover of life' and that fit Jeevanasen to a tee. We paid for an *ayah* (nanny) to take care of Hendrik while we were studying during the day.

We enjoyed Bangalore, and at an altitude of 3,000 feet its climate was pleasant. The time seemed to go quickly there, and by the time we had to sit for our First Tamil exam in early December, I had already caught up to the other missionary students who had been studying Tamil since January.

When David and Padma Gallup came to India in late 1959 as new missionaries to the Madurai-Ramnad Diocese of the CSI, they spent the next year at the language school in Bangalore. But in this case, only David studied Tamil while she taught it!

VATALAGUNDU

On December 11, 1956, Jane, Hendrik, and I moved from Bangalore to our first real home in India, Vatalagundu[1], located 30 miles west of Madurai and near the foot of the western ghat mountains. It was a town with a population of about 10,000 then. We moved into the western one-third of the mission bungalow located on a relatively large CSI compound just east of town. The whole of the bungalow was occupied in the very early 1900s by a single missionary family (Sherwood and Maud Eddy).

"Our" bungalow in Vatalagundu 1957

1. At that time, Vatalagundu was referred to as 'Batlagundu,' the English 'take' on the Tamil word.

It was a new age in the 1950s, and the church was still in the process of handing over the reins of the mission work more and more to Indian leadership. The missionaries themselves were tending to live in smaller, less ostentatious homes. The eastern third of the bungalow was the home of the Venkatasamis and their children; Mr. Venkatasami was the headmaster of the teacher-training school on the compound. The central one-third of the bungalow was part of the sleeping quarters for the teacher-training school students.

By the middle of January, after a month with no Tamil instruction, we obtained the services of our wonderful Tamil *munshi* (teacher), Y. D. Raja Rao. He moved from Madurai to Vatalagundu to begin teaching us. His job was to prepare Jane and me to take the second Tamil exam at the end of 1957.

We found a room for Raja Rao immediately adjacent to our part of the bungalow. He occasionally would eat with us, but usually, he would prepare his own meals. He had a huge capacity when it came to drinking South Indian coffee. (No wonder! It is *the* best coffee in the world.) One day he told me that he was often tempted to actually eat the instant coffee powder we used to buy; he loved the taste of coffee that much! Every day except Sunday, he would guide us through the beautiful intricacies of the Tamil language.

Our part of the bungalow consisted of four rooms—the room facing the broad veranda at the front of the house that we made into our sitting room and my office, an inner room with no windows, a dining room with kitchen, and the largest bathroom I'd ever seen. It had a backdoor leading to a courtyard used by the training school. A couple of months after we moved in, we had installed a very convenient Indian-style toilet at one end of the bathroom. After that, we didn't have to use the outhouse located about 30 feet from our corner of the veranda.

We slept on twin bunk beds upstairs. 'Upstairs' consisted of a single bedroom on top of our side of the bungalow's flat roof. We always kept the bedroom windows open unless there was a downpour. We had to tuck in mosquito nets under our mattresses after we crawled into bed to protect us from mosquitoes. We often could hear the hum of bats flying through the room over the mosquito netting frames on the beds. They were kind enough sometimes to deposit little black presents on top of the netting.

The training school boys gave us a lovely welcome as a part of a Christmas program they were giving one evening. We had our first taste of some of the fine Tamil music the boys were capable of. Before we arrived, the boys had whitewashed and cleaned the part of the bungalow we were to live in. Some evenings some of the boys presented what amounted to a Tamil jazz session, complete with beautiful drums and fired earthen pots used as percussion instruments. They were so talented, and we enjoyed the music very much.

We found there were many positive and exciting aspects of living in our new culture. The people seemed to have a characteristic easygoingness and slowness to anger. Even in crowds of poor and perhaps hungry people, there was order and good conduct.

The boarding school on the compound had an irrigated garden, and they gave me a little plot to grow vegetables. Many afternoons I would go there to check on my garden, and the old gardener who tended the school gardens would teach me how to plow with bullocks (oxen) and irrigate by drawing water from a well by bullock power.

The pastor for the CSI church in the compound, Rev. Ponnusami, used to teach Tamil to missionaries, so he was a big help in conversation when we would see him. He was a jolly, talkative man. He also served as the West Council's local Chairman, one of eight councils making up the Diocese of Madurai-Ramnad. He, therefore, supervised the work of the other pastors and lay evangelists in the council area.

There was a long-established boarding school for boys and girls on the compound, for first through eighth grades. Established by American Board missionaries, it was then receiving government support for teachers' salaries and some of the maintenance costs. It accommodated over 300 children, some of whom were day students from the town of Vatalagundu. Gradually all the elementary schools, government and religious, were being converted to *basic* elementary schools.

The teachers Basic Training School was only six years old when we moved there. It took boys who had at least an eighth-grade education. However, the following year, it started to only take boys with the equivalent of a high school diploma. When we were there, most of the boys were about 18 to 19 years old and came from poor village families. At that time, there were 40 first-year students and 40 second-year students. When they finished the two-year course, they had a good chance for employment in government or government-aided *basic* elementary schools. The headmaster, Mr. Venkatasami, was an alert and keen leader who was completely sold on *basic education*.

The students voted on their by-laws and met together monthly. They elected their ministers of food, agriculture, crafts, art and play, health, and finance. These elected ministers, together with their elected prime minister, made up the student governing council. There were certain hours every day given to work in the compound. Groups were rotated weekly to sweep, cook, serve, wash up, and irrigate and cultivate their two acres of land.

Discipline at the training school was fairly rigid. The boys rose at 5 AM, although those whose turn it was to cook rose at four. There were morning and evening prayers and six 40-minute class periods. In and out of class, the subjects dealt with were community training, cultural activities, agriculture, gardening, and cooking; teaching practice in villages; health, hygiene, and sanitation; spinning and weaving; educational psychology; *basic* education and school administration; and general teaching methods. The boys' success or failure was judged more by teachers' observation and judgment than by the examination at the end of the two years.

A few notable people visited us while we lived in Vatalagundu. The first was Raymond Dudley, the Secretary for India and Ceylon under the American Board of Commissioners for Foreign Missions (ABCFM). He was our boss, but one notch below the Bishop of the Madurai-Ramnad Diocese of the CSI. It was evident that he was happy to come and see us. But he seemed surprised by our youth, even though he was among several Board leaders who had interviewed me for the job 2½ years earlier in August 1954. Near the end of his visit, he remarked with a wry smile something taken from 1 Timothy 4:12, "Let no one despise your youth." Before Raymond became a regional Secretary under the Board, he had been an evangelistic missionary under the Madura Mission assigned to Aruppukkotai, about 30 miles south of Madurai.

The other distinguished guest, though hardly as prominent as she was later, was Gloria Steinem. She was 23 and showed up suddenly one morning, having taken a bus from Madurai. She stayed for lunch, and she was interested in what rural missionaries were doing in those years in so-called third-world countries. I don't recall anything particular about her personality nor her saying anything notably feminist.

Several times we were visited by Mr. J. E. Sokkiah when we were in Vatalagundu. He was a dear man of about 60 who had had several administrative posts in the American Madura Mission and, more recently, in the Diocese. He was comfortably chatty with us missionaries and had considerable respect for Raja Rao. He was a model of transparency and never tried to cozy up to either missionaries or officials in the Diocese to gain a better position. Instead, he proved to be very helpful to us in small ways, knowing he would not be compensated for it in any way, apart from mutual respect and friendship.

My only other work besides studying Tamil when we were in Vatalagundu was raising Leghorn chickens in a coop I had had built very near the bungalow. The aim was to give fertilized eggs, chicks, or pullets to the local people to raise their own flock of chickens. Unfortunately, I didn't have the chicken pen built so that it would keep out snakes. One morning when I went out to collect the morning's eggs, a snake began squirming out from under one of the nesting boxes. It was a cobra! So I tore into the house and seized my Sears garden shovel, one of the few U.S. tools I had brought to India. I rushed out with the shovel and into the pen. The cobra had not yet wiggled itself all the way out from the narrow space beneath the nesting box. I began hitting the snake with the back of the shovel. I was lucky, as after only a few blows, the snake was dead. I remember one of the elementary school boys nearby stating that I had committed a *pavam* (sin) by killing the snake; he had obviously been raised in a Hindu family.

One dark evening a few months later, however, there was a hubbub over in the teachers' quarters in the compound, about 100 yards from the bungalow. I went over to see what was happening. A cobra had been found in the courtyard in the back yard of one of the teachers' homes. There must have been a dozen male teachers there; several held bright kerosene pressure (Petromax) lanterns, and one had a rifle. They were trying to get in the right position so they could shoot the cobra. I must have stayed there for about an hour, still no dead cobra. I learned the next day that the teachers had been successful. They *had* to do it that night before the human occupants could go to bed, as the snake was caught between the front door of the house and the stout mud wall that surrounded the back yard.

Soon after moving into the bungalow in Vatalagundu, I walked the mile into town one afternoon to get postage stamps. On the way back, I was approached by a friendly stranger who invited me to have "coffee" with him. I accepted, and we turned into a little roadside Brahmin[2] 'hotel', meaning restaurant. Well, I found out it wasn't just having a cup of coffee. We started with one of the South Indian mouth-watering sweets, *kasari*, *jelabee*, or *lardoo*, followed by a savory dish, *vadai* or *pakora*, all on a banana leaf. These delicious dishes were followed by the star of the show—South Indian coffee—the best drink on God's green earth, complete with just the right amount of sugar and milk.

While we were devouring these delights, my new friend, Periyasami, asked me what crops are grown and what food we eat in America. He wondered whether we grew spicy chili peppers. I replied in Tamil that (at least at that time) little land in the U.S. was devoted to raising hot chili peppers. So he asked, "You don't have hot peppers with your food?" I said, "No." He queried, "Then how do you get any flavor with your food?" I said, "We have

---

2. There were many Brahmin 'hotels' in Tamil Nadu, but it didn't imply that you had to be of the Brahmin caste to eat there. It simply meant that they served vegetarian food, usually scrumptious vegetarian food. I always ate in Brahmin hotels when I was out.

other spices and salt and pepper to season our food." Periyasami simply couldn't fathom any meal without hot chilis. I had similar conversations during our first term with other rural people who also expressed disbelief about Americans' eschewing chili peppers.

After the tasty repast courtesy of Periyasami, we got up, and I thanked my new friend, and we parted. It was no surprise that I had no appetite for supper; I should have known it would be more than just a cup of coffee, as Periyasami had used the Tamil word for 'eat' (*sappidu*), not 'drink' (*kudi*) coffee!

In 1957, we went to Ramnad District, just to the east of Madurai District, to visit Ed and Fran Riggs for a week, missionaries under our mission. They served many villages there as an MD and RN, respectively. We decided to bring Raja Rao with us, as he was part of our family by then, and I didn't want to miss any of his lessons. The Riggses loved having him to help liven up conversations at mealtimes, including improving our knowledge about local history. Ramnad is a place with stunning Hindu temples and a few small English-style Anglican churches built by the SPG[3] before the Ramnad Protestant churches joined the Church of South India in 1947, a month after India formally obtained its independence from Britain.

On the whole, the Ramnad countryside presents a rather bleak and arid landscape with perhaps one *tank* (rain-fed reservoir) for irrigation available per village, and several sparsely-spaced palmyra palm trees yielding jaggery, an excellent substitute for molasses or sugarcane syrup, and toddy. (I took the photos of Raja Rao, shown in the first chapter of the **Epilogue,** when we were visiting the Riggses in Ramnad District.) Toddy is an alcoholic drink rarely imbibed when we were there, as Tamil Nadu was a dry state then. National Prohibition was advocated by Mahatma Gandhi, as well as by many Indian women. Prohibition, when implemented in India's states, led to lower rates of drinking among men and decreased incidence of violence against women. Nowadays, alcoholic drinks are banned only in the states of Bihar, Gujarat, Mizoram, and Nagaland.

---

3. Society for the Propagation of the Gospel in foreign parts (SPG) was a high-church missionary organization of the Church of England.

Ed and Fran Riggs and children in 1957

Fran and Ed and their three children lived very simply and were amazingly laid back. They were patient and loving with the people they had come to serve. While they had no vehicle other than ordinary bikes, a jeep would arrive on Saturdays at their village from Ramanathapuram, a small coastal town about 20 miles away, bringing supplies such as kerosene and foodstuffs. During our visit, I followed Ed one day on a bike to impromptu clinics; one was an outdoor clinic under a banyan tree just outside a village. I will never forget how expertly he performed his doctorly skills under less than ideal conditions and how skillfully he rode his bike on top of the one-foot-wide bunds that separated one farm field from the next. I, too, avoided falling over.

LIFE IN OUR VILLAGE

LIVING IN KALLIMANDAIYAM

Kallimandaiyam became 'Our Village' in October 1958 when we moved there from Vatalagundu—all four of us: Jane, Hendrik, Skyler, and me. The name Kallimandaiyam means a place with abundant milk hedge and a place to keep or herd sheep or goats. Milk hedge itself is a large, erect prickly shrub native to India's dry and rocky areas. We had wheels then, so that was good. Dick Keithahn had loaned us his old jeep while he was on furlough in the U.S. from October 1958 to October 1959.

Our village didn't have electricity for as long as we were there. We relied on kerosene as our only energy source apart from the sun. We had a regular range-sized four-burner stove that burned kerosene. And we had a small refrigerator that performed very well on kerosene, surprisingly enough. There was a petite freezer section of the frig, and using it, Jane was able to make ice cream.

At sundown, we would begin to light our ordinary kerosene lanterns. We also had one bright pressurized (Petromax) lantern, and we would usually fill it with kerosene and ignite it as the sunlight dimmed. It was relatively easy to read books even with small fonts with the light from a Petromax lantern. I used this light at night to do my project accounts and letter writing while sitting at one of our two desks.

Our new home was in a small mission compound at the edge of the village, which was little more than a wide spot in the road between Oddanchatram (9 miles south) and Dharapuram (16 miles north). The mission compound included an impressive little church consisting of only the sanctuary, a small L-shaped building intended to be a community center, and an elementary boarding school/orphanage that could accommodate 30 students.

We settled into the community center building as our home for the next two and a half years. It had four small rooms, one of which was our guest bedroom, where guests slept, and where for a time, we had to use to store boxes of U.S. surplus milk powder. The villagers around us needed the milk powder because one year the rains failed badly in our area during the rainy season. There was hunger among the landless *Dalits*[1], and we needed to help by distributing not only U.S. surplus milk powder but also sacks of surplus wheat, corn, and rice.

Catechist Samuel holding baby Skyler in courtyard of our home

Isaac (pronounced 'Eesāk') was a Christian Dalit from our village, and we hired him to do the essential tasks of hauling water, going shopping for us, and other miscellaneous jobs that would crop up.

He was a cheerful and faithful worker. He would haul the water we needed for the day from an eight-foot diameter drinking-water well located in our compound. Then he would pour the water into two concrete water tanks, one in our bathroom and one in the kitchen. On Thursdays, he would board a north-bound bus to go to the market in Dharapuram, 16 miles from us. There was probably at least one bus going either north or south every two

---

1. See the discussion of the Dalit people in the Prologue.

hours during the day. Isaac would bring us meat, usually chicken or mutton, duck eggs, other foodstuffs, and a large tin of kerosene. Duck eggs are nice and big and are just as tasty as chicken eggs, but we understood they were prone to carry paratyphoid bacteria, so we had to serve them hard-boiled.

Other than what Isaac would bring from Dharapuram, I was basically in charge of buying vegetables and fruit in Oddanchatram, which I passed through most days. Vendors would lay these wares down on large cloths spread out on the ground alongside the Dindigul-Palani road. I can remember buying mangoes, guavas, eggplants (actually egg size), tomatoes, and other veggies there and placing them in a sack in the jeep or in the saddle boxes on my motorcycle on my way home to Kallimandaiyam in the evenings.

Then there was the milk lady who lived in our village. Once or twice a week, she would suddenly appear inside our little courtyard and would announce her presence by yelling "Ayya!" or "Amma!" ('Sir' or 'Lady'). Sometimes she yelled particularly enthusiastically, in which case "Amma" turned into "Ammaaoo!" Her higher caste status and her innate fearlessness allowed her to treat us as complete equals, which we liked, unlike the Christian or Hindu Dalits in the village who treated us with far more respect than we believed necessary. The milk lady brought us milk from her water buffalo, which produced a good volume of delicious milk. We had to pay her on the spot (no monthly billing!), so we always had to keep some small bills around for that.

The milk was very high in cream content, so we would typically skim most of the cream off after it was refrigerated, and with that cream, Jane made tasty ice cream. The ice cream turned out to be a real hit, especially when we had guests, such as when fellow missionary Carol Weeber and Mrs. Tharien and her children from the Oddanchatram Christian Fellowship hospital visited us some Saturdays. Carol was a nurse, and once a month on Saturday, people suffering from leprosy from nearby villages would gather in our courtyard so Carol could give them their therapy pills for the month.

We hired Pappu (Mrs. K. Annapurani) to be our *ayah* (nursemaid) the whole time we were in the village. She was uneducated and couldn't even write her name, but she was brilliant. She could immediately sense what was the right thing to do in almost any social or work situation. She and her daughter, Chandra, lived with us. They slept in the far end of the dining room, separated from the main part of the room by a partition made of strips of palm leaves in a wooden frame. Pappu also had a son, Vadivel, who was in a boarding school, and he would come and be with us during vacations.

Pappu would not only look after Skyler but also shared the cooking with Jane. Pappu often referred to Skyler as her 'little clown' (*komalikutti*); he was born to be a truly funny guy. Pappu also washed our clothes, but Isaac's brother Gurumanikkum did the ironing. At age 30, Pappu was a widow, though she never divulged to us just what her husband died of. Hendrik and Chandra were close to the same age, and they would make up games using the simplest household items. The ground of our small courtyard consisted of coarse loose sand and was rather like a large sandbox, so that was a big plus in enhancing the enjoyment of playing outside.

The Kallimandaiyam area is probably the driest part of the Madurai district. From June through August, when the state west of Tamil Nadu, Kerala, was getting its monsoon rains, we on the eastern side only got strong dry westerly winds. In that season, the winds covered everything in our house with silty or fine sandy dust, which needed wiping off every couple of hours. Tamil Nadu and Kerala are separated by the Western Ghats (mountains), and since Kerala's monsoon comes from the southwest, as the moist warm air rises, it drops a lot of rain on the western side, but not on the eastern side. For us, monsoon rains usually came between September and December, but not always reliably. Most of the fertile fields in our area had to be irrigated by water from large-diameter irrigation wells ranging from 40 to 60 feet deep.

When we moved to the village, there was no electricity to power centrifugal pumps for irrigation. So the farmers used an old method for well irrigation wherein the farmer employed a pair of oxen (bullocks) combined with a system known as *kavalai*. A pair of bullocks is hitched so they can be driven down a ramp next to the well to pull a ~40-gallon metal container filled with water up out of the well. A 12-inch diameter 'tube' of leather is attached to the bottom part of the metal container. When pulled up to the top, the leather tube conducts water from the metal container into an irrigation channel next to the well.

As the bullocks are driven forward down the slope, the man doing the irrigation sits on two ropes, one connecting the bullocks to the metal container and one to the leather tube. The rope connected to the end of the leather tube travels over a wooden pulley at the ground surface. And the rope connected to the metal container rides over a higher pulley fitted on a wooden A-frame extending above the top of the well. The bullocks pull the metal container up to the upper pulley so it empties through the leather tube. At the same time, the leather tube is being pulled up and out over the lower pulley at the edge of the well, where it begins to empty into an irrigation channel. When the metal container is emptied, the farmer has to make his bullocks walk up that inclined ramp (backwards!) as the metal container with the leather tube is lowered back into the well. This is not easy for the bullocks or the irrigator (who must dismount and walk up the ramp himself). Then the cycle repeats. The photograph below illustrates the *kavalai* system of irrigation; however, in this case, the well is in the process of being dewatered to permit its deepening in the village of Andersonpatti. The work in Andersonpatti will be described later on.

Using *kavalai* system during deepening of large-diameter well at Andersonpatti

By the time we left India in 1961, electricity was just starting to come to our area. By that time, perhaps five percent of irrigated fields in our area were being irrigated utilizing centrifugal pump sets and the remainder still by the *kavalai* system. I remember hearing the squeaky pulleys of the *kavalai* system working in nearby irrigation wells, starting at 6 am, for perhaps two hours, and again for a couple of hours in the evening. The idea was to empty the well and then let it recharge itself in the next ten or so hours. Wells of this type could ordinarily irrigate only one to three acres using the *kavalai* system. But I saw many beautiful, flourishing small farms in our general area irrigated this way.

The village of Kallimandaiyam consisted of three small segregated neighborhoods. Opposite from us across the road to *Poruloor* was a Hindu Dalit community consisting of people who used to be called *Chakliars*. They made leather goods and also disposed of fallen animals, mostly oxen and cows. That's how they got the skins to process into leather. Catty-cornered from us across the road to Oddanchatram were the local Christian Dalits, who used to be called *Paraiyars* (sometimes known as the 'Sweepers' caste).

Traditionally they were musicians who played for weddings and funerals, but also traditionally, they had to dispose of the contents of chamber pots from those homes of higher-caste families.

Early on, I used to wonder how the Dalits of a village made a living. There was not enough leather tanning for the leather workers to provide for themselves year-round. There weren't enough special events for the other Dalits to provide for themselves by serving as musicians. Then I found out that each of the male Dalits in a village was usually associated with one of the Hindu farmers. The Dalits worked for the farmers in the fields and were also pretty much at their beck and call at other times. When the harvests came, each farmer would give *his* Dalit a share in the harvest.

Across the *Poruloor* road from us and southwest of the leather-workers community was the neighborhood where the caste people lived. They were mostly of the *Gounder* caste (farmers), a few *Chettiyars* (merchant caste), and some *Velalars* (landowners and officials). The *Gounders* were well known to be excellent farmers over a large part of Tamil Nadu. Trinity Baskeran,[2] a young Christian student pastor who worked with me in this village area during 1958–59, befriended a young *Gounder* man in the village, who was scheduled to be married but dreaded that day as in their tradition the groom's father slept with the bride on the wedding night. But as I learned later, he tied the knot anyway.

Kondarangimalai from our house

2. See the chapter on Baskeran later on.

Three miles to the east of us stood a stunning conical-shaped hill called *Kondarangimalai*, meaning 'the hill on which a cloud has descended' (கொண்டாரங்கி மலை) that rises a couple of hundred feet above an essentially flat plain. Geologically, the hill represents an anorthosite intrusion into the country granitic rock. A notable Hindu shrine complete with priest exists slightly below the peak. One Sunday afternoon, our family rented a bullock cart and driver to take us to the base of the hill. We climbed up to the top and greeted the priest. We took a picture or two and came down to our waiting bullock cart.

Two miles westward just off the road to *Poruloor*, there was a village populated by members of another caste, the *Kallars*. They had a strong reputation for being thieves. Many people believed that thievery was their caste job. Several people told me that these folks were the sole reason the Chief of Police of Tamil Nadu had decided decades back to place a police station in Kallimandaiyam. The police station was right in back of our little mission compound. *Kallars* were considered night-time robbers. A vaguely connected caste, the *Maravars*, living in Ramnad District, had a reputation for being *day*-time robbers, who were correspondingly bolder and more disposed to violence.

We never had a problem with the *Kallars*; they were mostly farmers and had land to farm in our area. One day a *Kallar* farmer came to see me in our home; he asked for a loan for his farm. I didn't have that much money to work with and decided that I wanted to help build up the Dalit peoples in our area. Later I considered the possibility that perhaps the *Kallar* gentleman was just 'casing the joint.' It's hard, though, to steal from a well-built home in Tamil Nadu, such as ours was, as there are closely-spaced steel bars in every window, and the doors can be locked shut during the night.

Most of the people in South India are said to be Dravidians, who are mostly dark-skinned. There is archeological evidence that the ancestors of present-day Dravidians populated an ancient civilization centered in the cities of Mohenjo-Daro and Harappa along the Indus River during 2500–1700 BC (in present-day Pakistan). One theory states that the Dravidian people may have been driven out of the cities of the Indus civilization by the Indo-Aryans[3] and wound up migrating to South India. Present-day Dravidians in South India speak at least one of the four Dravidian languages (Tamil, Telugu, Kannada, and Malayalam), which radically differ in terms of structure and phonetics from the Indo-European language Sanskrit. All the

---

3. But this Aryan Invasion theory has been replaced by most scholars by an *Indo-Aryan migration theory* based on detailed study of historical linguistics of the region, supplemented with archaeological data and anthropological arguments.

major north Indian languages, e.g., Hindi, Bengali, Punjabi, etc., are based on Sanskrit. Tamil is the native language to Tamil Nadu, formerly Madras State, and to the northern (Jaffna) area of Sri Lanka.

During April 1960, when the rest of the family was up in Kodai, I stayed back to do some work for a couple of weeks, and I attended the Friday evening service at our church in Kallimandaiyam. Afterward, Mr. Franklin, the headmaster of the CSI school there, asked where I was eating. I said in the local hotel.[4] He clucked his tongue and insisted that his family should give me dinner every night. I said that would be trouble for them because my return to Kallimandaiyam in the evenings was quite irregular. But he insisted. And I *was* grateful. The following Sunday at noon, they invited for the main meal too, so I went. It beat the one hotel in Kallimandaiyam by a wide margin. They served mutton with it, which was most tasty. I was surprised to hear they were able to get such good meat in Kallimandaiyam. I asked for the man's name who supplied the meat, and after my family returned home on the first of June, we started getting mutton from him. The Franklins lived in a single room with their three-year-old boy and their cute brand-new baby girl. They were undoubtedly cramped for space but never complained.

The local congregation took the celebration of Christmas very seriously. They whitewashed and decorated the church several days in advance. Every morning in the two weeks leading up to the day, the congregants went out together on the roads and sang hymns and lyrics (*bajans*) praising God for the birth of Jesus. On Christmas Eve, the Christians sung hymns, and with the help of loudspeakers, the music reached most of the village. The Christmas service commenced at midnight. Many worshippers remained in the church the entire night, saying prayers and singing hymns.

The 18-year-old son of Mr. Pandian Pillai, our village accountant (*Karnam*), died December 21, 1959. The boy had bone tuberculosis apparently for many years and had been quite sickly. We took a pot of tea to his grieving parents the next morning at their home. The father, who was the leading man of the village by virtue of his village accountant position, looked much shaken. The word *Pandian* of his name refers to an ancient Tamil dynasty existing in South India as early as 550 BC, and *Pillai* refers to his caste, *Velalar*.

In February 2011, forty years after we left India the last time for good in 1971, Skyler and I returned to India for a visit. We visited Kallimandaiyam late one afternoon and found that a CSI pastor and his family now occupied our old house (community center). We found Rev. Thangaiyah at home with his family, and we introduced ourselves to them. They were most hospitable to us. The Oddanchatram pastorate, formerly consisting

---

4. Restaurants are referred to as 'hotels' in much of South India.

of 50 congregations, had been divided up, and Rev. Thangaiyah currently pastored the 18 congregations close to Kallimandaiyam. He accompanied Skyler and me when the taxi we took from Palani drove us to see nearby villages I had worked in—Mandavadi and Navakani.

"Our" house in Kallimandaiyam as seen during 2011 visit

Rev. Thangaiyah, his children, and me at "our" house in 2011

Skyler and I noticed when we were sitting in the courtyard of our former home, now Rev. Thangaiyah's house, that a portion of the tile roof was badly in need of repair. So after we returned to the U.S., Skyler and I combined to send him a check to help him repair his roof. It took him a long time to cash the check, and we never heard any word from him at all. It was no doubt a mistake to send him the money, as the repair, in any case, would have been the responsibility of the Diocese. Rev. Thangaiyah probably felt diminished that a former missionary had paternalistically given him a handout that made him ashamed of the house he had to live in without sufficient funds to repair it.

BRIEF THOUGHTS ON HINDUISM

Some of the Tamil literature I had to study leading up to my third Tamil exam in 1959 was devotional literature from the *Shaivite* saints. A Shaivite is a devotee of the god Shiva, who is one of three main gods in the Hindu pantheon—Brahma, Vishnu, and Shiva—Brahma being the Creator, Vishnu the Preserver, and Shiva the Destroyer. But to a Shaivite, Shiva is not worshipped as the destroyer but is best characterized as the all-encompassing compassionate god, offering devotees the opportunity to worship and pray to him personally. This is one of the meditative (*Bhakti*) sides to Hinduism, for which Shaivite 'saints' have written hymns (600–800 AD), not unlike the Psalms in the Hebrew and Christian Bible.

Here is one of the many verses written by the Tamil Shaivite poet Manicka Vasahar:[1]

> O God! O spotless Gem!
> Thou didst enter my vile body,
> Melting and thrilling it
> With sweetness in every pore,
> Transforming it into
> A great and golden temple;
> And with ease hast made me thine!
> Thou Light that penetrated
> The confused entanglement
> Of trouble, birth and death!
> O my soul's delight!
> Hard after Thee I've followed
> And held Thee fast!
> Henceforth where wilt Thou
> Appear in grace to me?

1. White, *The Wisdom of the Tamil People*, 81.

There are also *Vaishnavite* saints and poets, Vishnu worshippers, for example, the Alvars in South India, who wrote similarly-sublime poems of praise during the same period expressing adoration to Vishnu and his avatars Krishna and Rama.

Hinduism is also practiced, probably by the majority, as a less meditative exercise and a more ritualistic religion associated with the priests and idols in their temples. Oaths are made by the worshipper concerning some offering or sacrifice to the deity to achieve some personally desired end. Worshippers also visit their chosen temple regularly to observe the *pooja* (worship) ceremonies performed by the priests at stated times during the day. Also, there are many roadside shrines containing particular idols, and private shrines are very common in homes, where householders can perform their own *pooja* rituals.

The nearest major Hindu temple from our village was the *Murugan* temple atop a hill inside the city of *Palani*, some 25 miles from our village by road. *Thai-Poosam*, considered the most important festival at the temple, is celebrated on the full moon day of the Tamil Month of *Thai* (January 15 to February 15). On this day, pilgrims, after first having taken a vow of abstinence, come barefoot, by walk, from distant towns and villages. Many pilgrims also carry a litter of wood or a pot of sanctified water on their heads, called *Kāvadi*, for the priests at the temple to conduct the *abhishekam* ritual on the holy day. For the three years we lived in the village, we used to watch, kind of awestruck, on the days leading up to the holy day, to see the many pilgrims doing *Kāvadi* walking south on the main road with a pot of water on each of their heads. They still had 25 miles to go as they passed our house.

OUR 'CLINIC'

As we were a Western white family living in a rural community far from a hospital, the poorest people just assumed that they could come to our home and have a fair chance of our taking care of their ailments. So we would have many people appearing in our little courtyard or on our veranda searching for some help with their ailments. Sometimes it just amounted to cleaning and dressing a wound. Sometimes it was something more serious.

Jane treated several men and women who were suffering from the Guinea worm. Most of the people she treated came from the village of Poruloor, about six miles west of us. That village had a drinking-water well that had fine-tasting water, but which also contained larvae of the Guinea worm, which when ingested allowed the larvae to grow inside the victim into adult worms. The larvae got into the well water when an infected woman got down into the well to collect water via steps cut into the side of the dug well. In the process, the woman's feet and lower legs would be submerged in the water allowing the Guinea worm larvae to come off of her legs and into the water.

Ten to fourteen months after a victim ingested water containing the larvae, a worm developed from a larva slowly migrates to the surface of the victim's body and emerges through the skin on the legs or feet, with great pain and disability in the process. When the adult worm is ready to come out, it creates a blister on the skin. Jane followed the advice she got from Carol Weeber and the doctors at the Oddanchatram Fellowship Hospital. As soon as a worm started to come out of a victim's leg, she very gently pulled the worm and, at the same time, wrapped it around a matchstick, and then dressed the area with a sterile bandage, covering the matchstick with the rolled-up worm.

Sometimes it took at least 5–7 daily visits like this before she was able to pull the worm all the way out. It was tricky business because if the worm broke during removal, it could cause intense inflammation as the remaining part of the dead worm would start to degrade inside the leg or foot. This would cause more pain, swelling, and cellulitis. Before we left India, I heard that local government officials had plans to drill or dig another drinking-water well in Poruloor, one that would not require the women to climb down into it.

Once around 8:00 after dinner, I had to pick up something from a little shop across the Poruloor road from us. So I walked across the road and bought whatever it was. On the way back, I felt as if my left leg had suddenly been cut or punctured as I was crossing the swale next to the road. When I got back to the house, we looked at what seemed to be minor cuts or punctures. We figured it could be that I just punctured myself on one of the thorny shrubs in the swale, *or*, it could be a snake bite, as we thought we could make out two possible snake-tooth marks on my lower leg. We decided to play it safe and treat it as a snake bite.

So Jane got one of my razor blades and proceeded to cut an 'X' at each of the two "tooth holes." She did her best to suck out the blood plus any snake venom from the incisions and then spit it out into a basin Pappu brought. We had no idea how to judge when we could safely stop the procedure; I guess it was when Jane got tired. And then we got into the jeep and drove to Oddanchatram, where Dr. Tharien gave me a shot of an anti-snake-venom serum. I felt fine through it all; it was probably nothing more than punctures from the thorny shrubs in the swale.

Many times people who came to our house for help with wounds or other health problems needed a doctor's attention. When we had Keithahn's jeep, I would take them to the Oddanchatram hospital. Failing that, I would put them on a bus to go to the hospital. In August 1959, I took a sick lady to the hospital. She had given birth to a healthy baby three days before. But as soon as I saw her I could tell she was in a bad condition. Dr. Tharien attended to her, but he was very pessimistic when he saw her. They gave her antibiotics and another drug all afternoon and night, but she died in the morning. Her husband, one of the poor Dalits, said that she had given birth to 19 babies, of which one older child and the recently-born baby were the only ones living. Such were the conditions.

VILLAGE ROWS

A couple of times I got involved in a village row. One early morning, we were awakened by a small group of people standing in our courtyard from a nearby village, Mandavadi. It seemed a couple in their village had had a row, and the wife decided she was leaving her husband and had left earlier that morning. That was not the worst part. The worst part was that she had left *with* the family cow. The people who had come to us were the husband's relatives. They thought we could *somehow* find the wife and the cow, and at least bring back the cow, if not the wife and cow together. The wife's relatives were also on their way to see us, we were told. Fortunately, we didn't have to mediate between the two groups, as the husband's relatives saw very soon, as we earnestly explained, that we had no power to bring the wife back, with or without cow.

This story seems humorous to *our* ears, but what it amounted to was the disaffected wife behaved very much like a few disaffected wives in the U.S. who first withdraw all the money from their and their husband's joint bank accounts and then take off to points unknown. The cow was probably the most expensive investment the couple had, with the possible exception of the very small house they lived in. But the cow was income-producing.

Another row that I, very unfortunately, tried to mediate happened right in our village a couple of hours after sundown one evening. Perhaps simmering beneath the surface for some time, a dispute had developed between the teachers at the CSI boarding school on our compound and the Christian Dalits of the village. We had already gone to bed when we heard a ruckus occurring in front of the church, right next to our house. The Local Council[1] Chairman from Dindigul, Rev. Williams, had apparently been notified of the problem and had come to try and deal with it peaceably.

---

1. There were six such Local Councils making up the Madurai-Ramnad Diocese.

But he and a couple of the teachers were arguing loudly in front of the church. Rev. Williams was taking the side of the local Christians. It didn't look as if it would end soon, so I rushed out in my bathrobe to "save" the day. One of the teachers had filled me in about the issue the day before, so before I said anything, I was kind of leaning toward the teachers' side. The spokesman for the local Christians let Rev. Williams speak for them. So then I began to "reason" with Rev. Williams about the issue. Not smart. In any case, without fully understanding the problem from both sides, I became the loser, as I lost some respect in the minds of both parties. On reflection later, I wondered if the issue just boiled down to caste considerations, assuming the teachers were of a higher caste than the local Christians and Rev. Williams, who were Dalits.

DIVERSIONS

Most of our diversions in the village were limited to writing letters home and reading, but occasionally something quite different presented itself to entertain us.

Twice we had a circus come to our village, and people from our village came to see it as well as those from the more interior villages. I think the circus was in our village for three or four evenings each time. They put up a tent, which was quite small compared to the circuses I attended as a boy. The main event in the tent I remember was an acrobatic cyclist who cycled all around the elliptical path in the tent and who was quite grim-faced throughout it all. But he was terrific and very much worth the entrance charge. And then there were the elephants which had come to our village by walking along the main roads with their mahouts. But they didn't do any tricks. They just wore colorful back coverings, and of course, strings of musical bells around their 'ankles'. While they were there, I can remember the sound of the elephant bells waking me up briefly whenever the elephants changed their position in the night.

Toward the end of our term, in late 1960 and early 1961, a traveling cinema started coming to our village quite frequently, a few days at a time. This involved setting up the big movie screen, the projector, and a loudspeaker system, directly across the main road from our house. The movies were all in Tamil, of course, and I attended a few. The problems for us were that the speaker system was set to a high volume and that the movies lasted until well after 11 pm. One had to be a very sound sleeper to sleep through it. As I was the lightest sleeper in our house, sometimes near the end of our term I had to take my motorcycle and drive the two miles to the CSI clinic in Mandavadi, where I slept quite soundly on the veranda of the clinic.

On two occasions, we took bullock cart rides for fun, though it's a very slow way of getting anywhere, and the ride is bumpy (no springs or shocks!). The first time was when we traveled east about three miles to see up-close the stunning conical-shaped hill, Kondarangimalai, as mentioned above. We climbed up to the top and greeted the Hindu priest there in the little temple. Then we came down to our waiting bullock cart.

Another day, I think it was on a Saturday, we went by bullock cart to a village, Keeranur, about three miles northeast of us, as we didn't have Keithahn's jeep any longer. We went at Rev. Selvaraj's invitation, the gregarious, cheerful pastor at the CSI church there. He wanted us to meet some of his congregants and enjoy dinner with them at his parsonage. We didn't see Rev. Selvaraj too often as the Keeranur parish was in the Coimbatore Diocese, just outside the Madurai-Ramnad Diocese boundary. We enjoyed being with them, and the dinner was delicious.

In early 1959 I was in Dindigul on business when I heard that the Prime Minister of India, Jawaharlal Nehru, was in town and would be speaking soon at the football grounds (Parade Ground) near the Tahsildar's[1] office. I drove over there in Keithahn's jeep and saw that quite a crowd had already formed. Presently, he appeared and started to give his speech, but I couldn't get very close because of the crowd, so it was a disappointment that I couldn't see him or hear him up close.

In July 1959, the whole family went by jeep to visit English Methodist missionary friends from language school, the Dobles, at their home in Udumalaipettai in present-day Tirupur district, 45 miles away. Udumalaipettai was well known as a hub for spinning and weaving textile production. We talked to the Dobles about their returning to England for good the following month because of Peter Doble's dysentery and very high blood pressure. So we wanted to say goodbye to them. We enjoyed the stay even though Peter made me preach Sunday morning's Tamil sermon and then conduct the whole evening English service for the Christian college staff and students there.

One Saturday night in September 1959, after we had given his jeep back to Dick Keithahn, Jane and I took a bus to Dindigul on an impulse. We went to hear a *kalakshepam* presented by a famous Christian singer. A *kalakshepam* is a Tamil sermon that is performed as a long song. It involves extolling the Christian message using the medium of South Indian Carnatic music. It was excellent; the preacher had a great voice.

One Wednesday in November 1959, we took a bus to Madurai to attend the new Indian bishop's consecration. His name was George Devadass, and

---

1. A *Tahsildar* was the highest government official in a *Taluk*, analogous to a township.

he had been a pastor in the CSI Madras Diocese. He was a calm, pastoral kind of man known for not taking sides in terms of caste positions or political parties, but he stuck to the demands of his conscience. He replaced Lesslie Newbigin, who had been our bishop since we arrived in India in 1956.

GETTING AROUND

In our village, there were several ways to 'get around.' The most common way for most of the poor villagers was simply to walk. Villagers in our area would think nothing of walking five to ten miles to go to an open-air market, a festival at a Hindu temple, the Oddanchatram Fellowship Hospital, or to our house to request some help from us.

Apart from walking, the most popular way of getting around in our local village area was by bicycle. Earlier, when we lived in Bangalore and Vatalagundu, our bikes were the only way of our getting around, apart from public buses. Our mailman in Kallimandaiyam delivered mail on his bicycle. Rev. Packianathan, our CSI pastor, living in Oddanchatram nine miles south of us, would visit many of his 50 village congregations on his bike. He was quite a heavy man, which made it that much harder, but I never heard him complain. Sometimes Trinity Daskeran, the student pastor assigned to our area, and I would visit villages in our area together on our bikes.

Then there were (and are) bullock carts, which were a relatively cheap way to ship goods provided you don't need them to arrive, say, at a town 50 miles distant overnight. But the carts ply along roads at their slow pace through much of the night, so comparing them to lorries (trucks, old chap), one needs to remember the story of the tortoise and the hare. Sometimes families can be seen crowded uncomfortably into a bullock cart traveling to a temple to attend a Hindu festival.

In rural areas, there were buses to carry you just about anywhere. Buses were reliable, and their drivers excellent. You could find them on routes with macadam roads or dirt roads. The average non-express bus did not travel very fast and generally stopped frequently to add or subtract passengers; in the bigger towns the wait at each stop was longer. Then there was usually at least a malodorous problem with the available public toilets at the bus stands. With express buses most of these problems disappeared, but the tickets were more expensive. When we lived in our village, bus fares were incredibly cheap, at least for us.

Speaking of bus tickets, these were generally sold by the conductor, just like on a train. You see, you get both a conductor and a driver with each bus. The conductor sells you the tickets and directs where people can sit to some extent, while the driver just drives. And then at stops, the conductor goes to a ticket kiosk and sells tickets to people who want to board there. If there is no bus ticket kiosk at a particular stop, the conductor just stands next to the bus and sells the tickets there.

One day in August 1959, when I was in the process of buying a ticket on an express bus from Oddanchatram to Madurai, I almost got literally crushed. In most cases, South Indians didn't get in line at ticket kiosks. They just congregated in a bunch close to the booth or kiosk, and the moment the conductor came and started to sell tickets for his bus, *everyone* just started surging toward the ticket kiosk. Those who could elbow their way to the ticket booth most effectively got there first and could purchase their tickets before the others. Sometimes, only a few seats were available, which meant that only the most successful pushers were the ones to get the few tickets. Most people understood what it meant to get in line (they called it getting in *queue*), but practicing it was just not ingrained in the culture.

In September 1958, when my missionary colleague Dick Keithahn was leaving on furlough to visit United Church of Christ churches in the U.S., he lent me his jeep to use until he returned the next year. It was a rugged vehicle of World War II vintage. It almost took care of itself, other than filling it with petrol (gas) and occasional servicing. But then I noticed one day that I could see daylight through part of the floorboard on the driver's side.

It appeared the floorboard was badly corroded. The nearest all-purpose auto repair shop was in Dindigul, a city 27 miles away by road. So I drove it there and discussed with the auto-body guy the process and price of basically replacing the floorboard on the driver's side. I wound up leaving it there and hoped the repair period would be short. It wasn't. I think I had to take the bus there at least two times to check on the work's progress before it was completed. (There were no text messaging, emails, or even telephones available to us then.) Maybe I could have sent him a return telegram from the Oddanchatram post office, but it didn't occur to me! After more than a month in the shop, it was finally done, and the floorboard felt and looked almost new. During the repair period I used my bicycle and public buses to get around.

The jeep was very helpful to me as I was beginning my work in our village area. I wound up giving lifts to many people known and unknown.

Also, I was able to take local government officials to villages that needed new drinking-water wells. They had money in their budgets for the wells, but they had no readily available transportation (other than public buses) to go and inspect the potential sites. On a couple of occasions, I took the Palani Tahsildar[1] himself and his assistant to several villages to inspect new water-well sites.

After Dick Keithahn came back from his furlough in September 1959, he took back his jeep, and for the following six months, I relied on my bike and public buses to get around. But in mid-March 1960, I was able to purchase an Indian-made motorcycle. It was a Royal Enfield 1.5 HP with lots of pep. It made a big difference when I had to dash from one government official to another, often in different cities. I particularly enjoyed it as in the evening I came home less fatigued.

One afternoon we headed for Oddanchatram on the motorcycle with Skyler in between Jane and me. We got there with no mishap and attended the program and prayer session the Christian Fellowship had there. But on the return, we were going past the village of Ambilikai on the way home when we encountered a pye-dog[2] right in the road. Poor thing it was so weak that it didn't respond to my urgent horn. So we hit it, and rather than the dog falling down, we did. Out of that, Jane got an abrasion on her left leg, and I got two on mine. Little two-year-old Skyler didn't have a scratch. But it was etched into his memory, for he kept saying for days on end, "Mommy, Daddy, Kalu (for Skyler) paw down motokaikul?" It took many days for Jane's and my abrasions to start to heal well.

But as with all newfangled devices and vehicles, I had my occasional mechanical difficulties with the motorcycle. Three months after I bought it, I lost about ten days because my motorcycle was first laid up for repair, and then I was. It started when I was cleaning the carburetor, and when mounting it back onto the block, I tightened one of the bolts too tight and the bolt broke off in the block. Then a day and a half later, after unsuccessfully trying to get the bolt out myself, I was on my way with the still-drivable motorcycle to get it fixed when I picked up a sharp bullock shoe in the rear tire, which resulted in a flat. I pushed the motorcycle back the 1½ miles to Kallimandaiyam.

Back home, after laboriously finally succeeding in taking the tire off the wheel (it was much more challenging than a car tire), I found I had punctured the inner tube in 20 places with my screwdriver. So off I went with the wheel by bus to Madurai to get a new inner tube and have it put

---

1. Township (*Taluk*) Manager located in Palani
2. An ownerless, half-wild, free-ranging dog that lives in villages

on. I came back that night with a decent used tire and a new inner tube installed. In the morning, when I had almost finished putting the wheel on, I accidentally pulled the machine down on the ground, and in the process, the still-unfastened rear brake rod got bent and broke off.

After a few moments of rage, off I went to Dindigul to have it repaired with only my front brake working on the way. I was going slowly, and when I got to Oddanchatram I went even slower. Still, when a cyclist came in front of me suddenly, and he didn't pay any attention to the noise of my motorcycle, I found that I could only keep from hitting him by allowing the motorcycle to fall over. That I did, and I got off with only a few abrasions on my legs and a slight burn on the right leg. After a brief treatment of the wounds at the Oddanchatram Fellowship Hospital, I proceeded to Dindigul, and the mechanics there spent from 2 pm until 2 am the next morning on the bolt that had broken off in the block. They finally succeeded, bless their persistent souls, and they even left the inner thread intact. And then they lost no time in welding the brake rod back to its normal position.

Since then, the motorcycle behaved itself quite decently. However, going against the wind was a bit hard sometimes for its 1.5 HP engine, and I sometimes had to shift from third to second even when I wasn't going up an incline. Such are the terrible winds of this great land.

As an encore to this series of events, I found that my leg abrasions and the burn on my right leg had become infected, so I had to go to the Oddanchatram hospital to get a penicillin shot. Then I settled myself for a long 'winter's rest,' because I remembered a recent time when my leg got infected and I didn't stay indoors. It took quite a time to get healed. So, I was a homebody for a few days, and I caught up with my correspondence and accounts, and we four enjoyed each other's company again. When I had sufficiently healed, I started wearing a *dhoti*[3] every day. It seemed natural, more modest, and gave me a little more protection for my legs than my shorts.

I concluded that the more sophisticated the transportation mode, the more it seems like a necessary evil. I also figured that having a motorcycle is still better than having a horse for transportation, as I avoided the injuries from any stout kick from a horse, which could have been far worse than my minor skin abrasions and burns.

---

3. A *dhoti* extends from the waist down to one's chappels (similar to sandals).

RAMESH

K. Ramesh, taken during our 2011 visit

It was amazing how we met K. Ramesh. After my family and I left for India in 1956, my mother and dad in Detroit became interested in India. My dad, a family practitioner himself, befriended a couple of Indian doctors in the city. Then my parents started having those doctors and their families over to dinner, and the Indian friends reciprocated. Ramesh attended at least one of the dinner parties and was introduced to my parents. He was an Indian student at Wayne University in Detroit (now Wayne State University).

Ramesh finished his bachelor's degree in the fall semester of 1959–60 and was planning to fly back to India via Germany. On the day in February 1960 when he had emptied his apartment and was packed up ready to leave, he started to feel ill. Then he began to feel *really* ill with a fever. He didn't know what to do, but finally he decided to call my dad, which he did. Dad went to his apartment and examined him. He told Ramesh, "You are in no condition to travel," and dad then drove him to our home. Mother welcomed him and the two of them were able to get him upstairs and into bed in the guest room, where Ramesh just passed out and slept for many hours. The diagnosis was pneumonia. Mother nursed him back to health and dad administered the appropriate medications to him. In a few days his health had improved at least sufficiently well so he could board a plane and fly back home to India.

In a recent unsolicited email from Ramesh, he wrote me that he would always remember with the greatest gratitude the care he was given by my mother and the way both my parents treated him like a son. "Those words, and their care, are still ever green and overflow with gratitude for their outlook and their treatment to me when I needed help in a foreign land." In August 1987, I invited Ramesh to attend my mother's 90th birthday party at her retirement home in Philadelphia. I was amazed and delighted when both he and his wife Soumini came. As he recently wrote, he was able at that time to talk to my mother and "take her blessings."

It turned out that Ramesh was from South India, not only South India, but he was actually from the city of Madurai, the capital of the district where I was working!

One afternoon in May 1960, when we were vacationing in Kodai, who should wake me from a deep nap but Ramesh and his cousin Ram! We were so happy to meet him after receiving the letter about him from Dad and Mother; we liked him immediately. The next day, he came by and invited me to play golf with him, which he was just picking up. So I agreed, and we did have fun on Kodai's golf course, even though it had been 12 years or so since I had last played. He also took me to see the two elegant TVS guest houses in Kodai owned by his family.

We soon learned that Ramesh belonged to a wealthy and successful family. His grandfather was T. V. Sundram Iyengar, the last name indicating that he was a *Vaishnavite Brahmin*, a worshiper of Vishnu and his avatars Krishna and Rama. In 1911, T. V. Sundram Iyengar founded T. V. Sundram Iyengar and Sons [Pvt Ltd], a bus company in Madurai which later diversified into automobile production and emerged as the parent company of the TVS Group, now one of India's most prominent business conglomerates. Ramesh's grandfather had five sons and three daughters, and in his patriarchal Tamil *Brahmin* family, all the sons, including Ramesh's father T. S. Krishna, joined their father in the business.

The TVS group established by Sundram Iyengar is currently the largest automobile distribution company in India with 30 subsidiaries in many diverse fields: automotive component manufacturing, automotive dealerships, fasteners, and textiles manufacturing, as well as financial, electronics, and IT solutions services, to name just a few. The group is reported to have an annual turnover of about $8.5 billion, with employees numbering more than 60,000. Some of their manufacturing business projects in the last decade or two have extended to other countries.

T. S. Krishna, Ramesh's father, served as Managing Director of the TVS Group in the 1960s. When Ramesh returned from Detroit with his bachelor's degree in January 1960, his father immediately put him to work on the floor of the large TVS auto repair facility in Madurai. Krishna wanted him to learn the business from the ground up by working with the mechanics (technicians), and he did. Presently Ramesh is the Managing Director of *Southern Roadways*, which has provided reliable bus service and lorry transport service throughout South India for many decades. He also serves as one of the Directors of the TVS Group itself and two subsidiaries.

One of T. S. Krishna's sisters, T. S. Soundram, Ramesh's aunt, played a significant role in the independence movement under Gandhi. At age 32, as soon as she graduated as a medical doctor in 1936, she threw herself completely into the freedom struggle and worked directly with Gandhi. As freedom neared, Gandhiji decided she would serve India better by not getting involved in politics. Impressed with her commitment, he made her the representative in South India of the Kasturba Gandhi National Memorial Trust. And he entrusted her with setting up an institution in a rural area that would improve the lives of the poorest people.

Thus was born the idea of Gandhigram, where villagers would be taught skills and provided support to revive village industries and the rural community's economy. Along with her husband, Dr. G. Ramachandran, she founded Gandhigram and the nearby Kasturba Hospital in 1947 as a memorial to Kasturba Gandhi, Gandhi's deceased wife. It was located just six miles southeast of Dindigul then in Madurai District. Soundram dedicated herself to this project that focused on healthcare, education, economic development, and social welfare in the rural communities of the surrounding area.

At this very time in 1947, Dick and Mildred Keithahn, as missionaries of the ABCFM, returned from the U.S. and were invited by Soundram to help with the development of Gandhigram.[1] Dick worked there with Soundram and her husband from 1947 to 1956, the year the Millses appeared on the scene.

I know from personal experience that TVS ran Southern Roadways like a well-oiled machine, like clockwork. Every time I went to their large repair garage in Madurai, I wondered at how clean it was and how polite and efficient the managers and staff were[2]. The TVS family has always prided themselves on maintaining fair and decent treatment of all their employees.

Since our years in India, Ramesh has been most generous and hospitable to me and my family members who have come to India to visit the country or give ourselves a refresher course on places and people we have known. Ramesh has even provided us with a car and driver to take us anywhere in South (or North!) India. It is always a pleasure to renew our friendship with him.

Ramesh had two brothers, Suresh and Mahesh, and a sister, Radha. Like Ramesh, his brothers took active roles and significant responsibilities in the TVS Group. Unfortunately, Mahesh, Ramesh's younger brother, passed away in January 2019. He had been Chairman of Sundram Brake Lining Ltd, while Suresh is still Chairman and Managing Director of TVS Sundram Fasteners in Chennai (Madras).

Ramesh's sister Radha, it turned out, was getting ready to get married very soon after we met Ramesh for the first time in May 1960.

---

1. See the chapter about Dick Keithahn in the Epilogue.
2. In 2011 when my son Skyler and I visited Ramesh in India, he gave us a tour of one of TVS's fasteners factories a few miles south of Madurai. It was immaculate and beautifully designed and run.

RADHA'S WEDDING

On Wednesday, June 29, 1960, one of the windiest days we had in Kallimandaiyam, who should drive up to our home in a Fiat but K. Ramesh with a personal invitation to his sister's, Radha's,[1] wedding the following Monday (July 4th). That was the only reason he drove the 63 miles out from Madurai and back again! I told him that I had already scheduled my North Local Council Rural Work committee at Dindigul for the fourth, the same day as the wedding. Then as he kept urging us and mentioned that there would be classical Tamil music and classical dancing at the reception, I became much more inclined to postpone the committee meeting. And also, as I witnessed his partaking with us of our ordinary supper, possibly mixed with the red dust deposited by the wind that afternoon, just to bring us the invitation, we agreed that we would try our very best to come.

The next day, I sent out postcards changing the meeting date from the fourth to the fifth of July. On Saturday, Ramesh sent me (as a present to me for attending his sister's wedding) two high-quality four-yard sheer cotton dhotis. I had no proper dress-up Indian-style shirt (called a *jibba*) that would match one of the elegant dhotis, so I had a *jibba* made out of the second of the dhotis by a tailor in Oddanchatram soon after church on Sunday. Jane got out some lovely pink drip-dry material my mother had sent her, and she had it made into an attractive maternity dress to wear to the wedding.

Then late afternoon on Sunday, we took my motorcycle with our suitcase tied to the back and headed for Oddanchatram, where we failed to board the Palani-Madurai express bus as it was full. Back we crawled onto the motorcycle and made our way to Dindigul and pulled up to the bus stand there and the last TVS bus to Madurai was almost ready to leave.

---

1. The goddess Radha for whom the bride was named is worshipped as a deity of love, tenderness, compassion, and devotion.

There was room for two, so I put Jane on the bus, drove the motorcycle around the corner to the CSI pastor's house, parked it there, ran back, and boarded the bus just as it was pulling out. We got into Madurai about 10:15 pm, and the Kellys,[2] our hosts at American College[3], though they had given up on us, gave a fine welcome and even treated us to a dinner of chicken on toast. We *had* to get into Madurai that evening because we had to be at the wedding by 8:30 the next morning.

I felt nervous on Monday morning when we were waiting for Ramesh to send a car to take us to the wedding. I had never before worn such elegant looking clothes in my life. It made me feel slightly out of my role. Anyway, the car came, and we went to the wedding on the grounds of his large house in another part of Madurai. We were hardly noticed by any of the many guests. So we weren't subject to much staring as I feared. Ramesh's family had sent out over ten thousand invitations to the wedding.

There must have been at least 50 Brahmin priests to solemnize the Hindu marriage during the morning and perform the required rituals. Mr. Krishna, Ramesh's father, wore nothing but his dhoti and a sacred cord around his neck during the whole ceremony. He played a big part in it until the *tali* (marriage necklace, like a wedding ring to Westerners) was tied around his daughter's neck.

Many rituals were impossible for me to understand and many more spoken in Sanskrit, the meaning of which was indeterminable by me. It's possible that many of the rituals were not entirely understood by even the bride, groom, or the parents. Anyway, it was all fascinating and pleasurable. The bride, Radha, was nineteen and seemed to be a very nice, natural girl. I understood that she used to go weekly to Ranchanyapuram, a CSI compound a little north of Madurai, and help the girls at the school make dolls and similar things. Imagine, the daughter of T. S. Krishna doing things as helpful and ordinary as that!

At noon they began feeding about 7,000 people, including us and all the TVS workers, mechanics, bus drivers, etc. What wonderfully delicious vegetarian dishes they served, unlikely to be found anywhere else on this planet. Also, very well-placed people were there as guests, including the

---

2. Bill and Karen Kelly were missionaries under the UCBWM, as were we; he served as chaplain to the college.

3. The American College is a well-respected Christian college in Madurai established by missionaries of the American Madura Mission. It is largely independent of the Madurai-Ramnad Diocese.

Chief Minister of Madras State (now Tamil Nadu) and the famous Tamil movie star Sivaji Ganesan[4].

It was all really elegant as a Hindu wedding, and everything was wonderfully and elaborately decorated. It was more like a state fair, what with the many large *pandals*[5] and temporary buildings put up and all the vacant properties near the TVS house set up for serving food. I thoroughly enjoyed it all, especially since the whole thing was done in taste, and it offered high-class entertainment for so many people. I was sure the family didn't have to go into debt just to put on a big show, which is the case with many Indian weddings involving middle-class families.

The reception began at 5:30 pm, which included an entertainment program consisting of *Carnatic* music with the best singer, the best violinist, and the best drummer in South India. It was terrific—much more disciplined and intricate than jazz but with the similarity of frequent on-the-spot improvisations. That part of the program lasted until 8:30. About 9:30, the dance performance, *Bharata Natyam,* began, featuring Kamala Lakshmi, then the best dancer of this art form in South India. Bharata Natyam is a major form of Indian classical dance that is indigenous to Tamil Nadu.

This day had to be one of the many high points of our first term in India.

---

4. I swear Sivaji Ganesan starred in at least 90 percent of the Tamil movies made in Madras, and they were many.

5. A shelter of upright poles supporting a roof that is usually made of palm-leaf matting

THARIEN

In 1955, Dr. A. K. Tharien, his wife Mariamma and a nurse, Kunjamma, set up a small clinic and hospital in Oddanchatram, just three years before my family and I moved to nearby Kallimandaiyam. Tharien was 35 years old. The idea for forming a Christian medical fellowship to serve a medically needy rural area in India was born in a prayer group that formed when Tharien went to medical college at Miraj in Maharashtra in central-western India. Many members of that prayer group dedicated themselves to serve together as doctors or nurses in a poor village area.

Dr. A. K. Tharien in 1984

After completing his studies at Miraj, Tharien went to the Stanley Medical College in Madras to complete his medical training. Soon after, Tharien and Mariamma went to Kanchipuram, and he later became the medical superintendent of the Church of South India hospital there. Kanchipuram is a famous temple city in Tamil Nadu, located about 50 miles west of the city of Madras (Chennai). But Tharien remembered the promise he made to God at the Miraj Medical College, which made him rethink his comfortable salaried position. He and his wife prayed for guidance to choose the right rural area to serve the poor.

The Oddanchatram Christian Fellowship Hospital (CFH) started in a small house right along the main road to Dindigul that nurse Kunjamma had rented as an advance party. Initially, the house owner didn't collect rent because the place was said to be haunted[1]! But that did not deter these dedicated Christians. Very soon after the Thariens and Kunjamma started their work, new members, who had taken the pledge in fellowship, arrived to serve as doctors, nurses, pharmacists, and lab technicians, and the hospital grew. Most of the members of the Fellowship were Malayali Christians, meaning they spoke the Dravidian language Malayalam and hailed from the southwestern-most state, Kerala. Despite their different mother tongue, they all became quite adept at speaking Tamil.

Tharien and Mariamma surrendered their entire personal material possessions and bank account to the Fellowship for the initial purchase of properties and to meet the expenses to start the hospital. From the startup of the CFH, members of the Fellowship accepted mutually agreed-upon subsistence compensation for their work, and they shared many things in common.

The hospital's philosophy has been to provide the best medical treatment onsite and in several nearby village clinics with fees as low as possible. When we were there, they charged fees that were graduated depending on the patient's family's ability to pay. Desiring to be self-supporting, the Fellowship has eschewed accepting funds from overseas, although there have been a few grants from foreign charitable organizations they have received for specialized purposes.

Since its beginning in 1955, the hospital and its services have experienced remarkable growth. They now have 25 members of the Fellowship, who direct the hospital's operation and look to expand the services they offer in nearby villages. The staff, including trainees, numbered 568 in 2019, and the hospital had 300 beds. The hospital buildings are many now, and the Fellowship provides several training programs, including a College of Nursing, Masters in Family Medicine, and diploma training in medical lab technology, medical records technology, and radio-diagnosis technology.

Before he died in Oddanchatram on April 23, 2006, Tharien became well known and respected in medical circles and peace groups. He advised

---

1. Our Jeremy was born in the second floor of that house five years later on October 19, 1960.

the World Health Organization on medical ethics. While being an ardent Christian, he was an admirer of Gandhi and a firm believer in non-violent approaches to conflict situations. He was active in peace organizations and, at one point, led an international peace delegation to the United Nations. Whatever group he worked with, he was admired for his courage of convictions and his honesty. The source of his faith was his prayer life. He and Mariamma would start and end each day with prayer together.

When I was in Kallimandaiyam during 1958–61, I visited the hospital and Tharien and Mariamma quite often. They always welcomed me warmly. Their three children were wonderful: Susheel, Prakash, and Nirmala. Susheel became a medical doctor, as did Nirmala. Susheel and his wife joined the Fellowship many years ago, and he serves as the chief psychiatrist on the hospital staff. Nirmala married a medical doctor, and the two of them, I understand, have performed outstanding Christian service in many remote parts of North India and, more recently, in Papua, New Guinea. When I last heard, Prakash and his wife and children were living in Mangalore on the west coast of India.

The CFH was important to us for our own health needs: physical checkups for our children, treatment of our infected abrasions and burns, and my treatment for a possible snake bite. Jane gave birth to Jeremy on the second floor of the original 'haunted' house under the care of Dr. Mary Cherian. She and her husband, Dr. Jacob Cherian, were two of the early members of the Fellowship. Two years after we returned to India in 1967, Dr. Tharien took out Hendrik's tonsils.

Tharien and Mariamma were probably the most dedicated Christians I have ever met. Both were kind and gentle and very hard workers. There was no doubt that Tharien was full of love for all his brothers and sisters in this world. And he showed it in his care for his patients and the way he greeted and hosted friends and strangers. I visited them and stayed with them when I made short visits to India with Jeremy in 1984 and with Hendrik in 1991.

After we returned to the U.S. in 1961, I kept in touch with Tharien through letters. One time when I wrote to him, I addressed him as "Dear Dr. Tharien." He let me know in his reply that such a salutation was far too formal. He said that he wanted the warmer "My dear Tharien," which I adhered to after that.

Tharien made trips overseas several times, either to attend conferences and give speeches on medical ethics or medical practice in poor areas, or to meet with leaders of peace organizations, for example, in Japan and the U.K. In 1965 when I was studying at the University of California at Davis for an advanced degree, I heard that Tharien was coming to the U.S. and was to speak in several cities. I wrote to him and asked if he could come to Davis also. I would set up opportunities for him to speak at our church and the university, if possible. He agreed, and I found the money to pay for his extra stopover. Of course, he stayed with us during his visit, and it was wonderful seeing him again and having him with us. I always admired Tharien and Mariamma so much.

Sarah David, a member of the CFH 'family,' wrote Tharien's obituary, in which she included the following:

> Many thoughts ran through my mind. The picture of his walking the hospital pathways, his gentle smile lighting up his face, his enquiring about family, the hospitality at home, his usual place in the chapel, and his ready invitation always to work at CFH. All of these spoke so much. Then there were the notes of encouragement he wrote. . .could not forget Amma too. Together they blessed our lives quietly.
>
> Seeing him lying in his coffin, with so many paying their respects, the rich, the poor, the lame, government officials, the police department, all alike sharing their grief. It overwhelmed us.
>
> Ayya, as we lovingly called Dr. Tharien, received many accolades and honours during his lifetime, yet the one that stood out above all, I think, was the one that called him home to his Lord, "Well done, good and faithful servant. . ."

In February 2011, when Skyler and I visited South India, we stopped by Oddanchatram and visited the hospital. It had grown into a city-sized hospital, and I didn't know my way around. Finally, I was able to send word to the then superintendent of the hospital, T. Susheel, Tharien's older son. He was then the medical superintendent of the hospital. He met us and kindly took us on a tour of the greatly expanded hospital and grounds. He showed us the burial stone indicating where his father and mother were buried.

CAROL WEEBER

Carol Weeber, hailing from Beaver Falls, Pennsylvania, was a nurse in the American Madura Mission who worked during her first term at the Mission's hospital in Madurai. When she returned from her first furlough in 1954, she decided she wanted to work in public health in a medically-needy rural part of Madurai District. After prayer and discussions with Bishop Newbigin and the American Board, she proceeded with the plan and chose to move to Oddanchatram. Very soon she found a few Indian friends to assist her in her mission, and they formed her 'family' and lived together with her in an old two-story house close to the main road. They established a clinic and soon were presented with many people coming every morning for medical help. Hers was the only medical center of any kind in the 36 miles between Dindigul and Palani.

Carol Weeber, courtesy of her nieces and nephews

Sometime after the Christian Fellowship Hospital was established in Oddanchatram the following year, Carol decided she and her 'family' would move seven miles down the road to the village of Chatrapatti. She didn't leave Oddanchatram because the Christian Fellowship had come to town, but because of an interesting conflict she had with her landlord in Oddanchatram. It seemed, from her autobiography at any rate (*In Lifting Get Under*[1]), that her landlord had asked her to allow him to boil milk on her stove in the house. But she believed that the boiling of milk in his (Hindu) religion was an act of worship to an idol-god, and she refused his request. The next week he told her to vacate. As she couldn't find other suitable quarters in Oddanchatram, she found one in Chatrapatti and moved there.

She and her 'family' continued their clinic work there, but also Carol began the significant work of befriending poor children of all ages and helping them get an education. There were street boys back in Oddanchatram, and she set up an informal school for them and helped them with nutritious meals.

Sometimes she helped the children by paying for their tuition at mission boarding schools in Kallimandaiyam, Dindigul, or Madurai. At other times, when the children were accepted at free government schools, they were still required to buy their uniforms, school supplies, and a 'tin' trunk for holding the school supplies. Carol helped with that.

I remember Carol coming in her jeep to Kallimandaiyam once a month on Saturday afternoons. She'd set up shop in our little courtyard, where she would attend to a short line of leprosy patients who had walked or come by bullock cart from nearby villages. In addition to tending to any other health concerns they may have had, Carol would give them a month's supply of tablets of the drug *dapsone* as well as multi-vitamins. The drug could kill the bacteria that caused the disease, thus stopping any ongoing progress of the disease. But there was no way to turn back the often grotesque disfigurement of hands and feet it had already caused unless reconstructive surgery developed by Dr. Paul Brand in the early 1960s could be performed. Unfortunately, in the 1960s, medical practitioners found that the specific villainous bacillus was developing resistance to *dapsone*.

Leprosy, also known as Hansen's disease, is caused by a bacillus, *Mycobacterium leprae*. It's been around for centuries and centuries, as indicated in the literature of ancient civilizations. In the past, people afflicted with it were often ostracized by their communities and families, as evidenced by the presence of leper colonies in several countries, only a few of which exist today.

---

1. Weeber, *In Lifting Get Under*, 85.

Now we know that leprosy is not very contagious. You can't catch it by touching someone who has the disease. Most cases of leprosy are from long-term contact with someone who has the disease. But it remains one of the leading causes of deformity (usually of the hands and feet) from an infectious disease in the world. Over four million people live with leprosy-related disabilities, and it remains one of the leading causes of long-term nerve damage in the world.

India now has the highest incidence of leprosy globally, with an average number of new cases of 120,000 to 130,000 per year. Between 1985 and 2015, new cases of leprosy in the U.S. ranged from 80 to 350 annually. Today it is curable using multidrug therapy, which has a low chance of the bacillus developing resistance to it. The incidence of the disease *is* slowly declining in most countries of the world, a direct effect of widespread administration of the multidrug therapy by public health workers. But identifying and monitoring resistance to the treatment are still necessary as the disease continues to emerge.

Carol was a trip. No matter what circumstance she was in, she always had a ready smile and interesting comments on related topics or the world's latest happenings. The only thing that might motivate her to anger was if someone lied or proved untrustworthy. She had a great sense of humor, and she immersed herself more than most missionaries in the lives of the poorest people. She had a great interest in so many things and was always optimistic. One time Carol was telling Jane about a few people's poverty she had met and was trying to help. Jane, consistently pessimistic, responded, "Why would these people even want to *live*?" Carol's quick retort was, "Why, they very *much want* to live!"

Carol and Jane agreed on one thing, though. They abhorred using words designating a person's caste, such as 'Velalar' for a particular high-caste group or the word 'Harijan' implying an outcaste. They thought that using such terms, even in private, would imply approval of the caste system and would only promote more caste-based divisiveness. I think they were right. But at the time, I felt that learning a person's caste was interesting and often helped me understand the dynamics of interactions I witnessed. But I would never mention anybody's caste when talking to others or modify my demeanor based on the caste of any person I was talking to. At least I hoped so.

In 1965 Carol left the Madura Mission and moved to Salem District, also in Tamil Nadu, about 90 miles north of Chatrapatti. There she joined the Hill Gospel Fellowship, whose purpose was to evangelize the hill tribal people there. And in 1976 Carol moved again, this time to North

India. From 1976 to 1992, she served at missionary children's homes in Bhogpur and Roorkee, in or near the foothills of the Himalayas. When Carol was ready for retirement in 1992, the Christian Fellowship in Oddanchatram invited her to reside in their hospital compound, where she spent a few months. But then she decided to come back to the States via Madras. She stayed for some time with her sister in Bethlehem, Pennsylvania. That's when I helped her with editing a portion of her book *When Lifting Get Under*.

When I recently reread her book, she mentioned an activity of mine in 1960 I had forgotten about. It happened in the village of Boduvarpatti, not easily accessible from the main road connecting Oddanchatram and Palani. The new Christians of the village needed a drinking-water well, and I applied several times to the Tahsildar in Palani for the funds for digging a well for them. Despite all that, the approval never came.

At about the same time, I had heard of some forest land in the Palani hills' foothills, which had been clear cut, and the government had planted saplings of Senthanagu trees, the wood of which was ideal for match sticks. The government planned to settle landless people close to this plantation where they could protect the trees from poachers and, at the same time, earn a living by raising crops in the open spaces between the tree rows. When the trees matured and were ready to harvest, the government would sell the trees to the highest bidder.

One night at a meeting in Boduvarpatti, I presented this opportunity to the landless Christians, which they were immediately enthusiastic about despite my warning them that water would likely be a problem there. I remember the day we took Ponniah and a few other representatives of the congregation up the forest road to look at the site, along with a government forest officer. Once they saw the site, these few decided that all of their congregation would move there. I later heard that the congregants did in fact move there and hung on in that forest area working the land for several years. And later, they moved 20 miles farther from their native village to a Christian agricultural center, where their prospects were brighter.

After my family and I left India in April 1961, Carol and Rev. Packianathan would visit the Boduvarpatti congregation to hold services when they lived in the forest area. Carol also took over from me the responsibility of distributing U.S. surplus milk powder, cheese, wheat, and cooking oil in her area, as if she needed another job!

Over her life of service in India, I have never known anyone to care so little for her own comfort as Carol. She would gladly embark on a frequently uncomfortable trip, often at the drop of a hat. By bullock cart, by train in third class, by cycle rickshaw, by bicycle over rough pathways, often at considerable distances. All to accompany students to schools, attend to a sick person, participate in preaching the gospel to hill-tribe people, be present at a person's graduation, or a couple's wedding. And behind all this was the broad love she had for the poor people she met, whom she often knew quite personally.

WORK CAMP

In the third week of May 1959, I took part in a week-long work camp in Oddanchatram sponsored by the Student Christian Movement of India. Twenty students (young men) built a simple earthen building with wood framing and a thatched roof to provide a home for boys ('Street Boys') who were routinely sleeping on the streets of Oddanchatram. As noted above, Carol Weeber had taken the street boys as one of her concerns, and because of this need, the idea for the work camp was born. During the day, the students would do the building work, and in the evenings there were inspirational speakers and discussions on the role of Christians in society.

One evening, Rev. Joseph John spoke to the boys. He had established a model agricultural community near Madras that included a well-functioning farm and a Christian fellowship. When Jane and I visited his village in 1957, which he had named Deenabandhupuram (village of the servants of the poor), we were able to attend our first Muslim wedding because of the cordial relationships Joseph John had established with Muslims (and Hindus) in the neighboring villages.

One day, Dr. Tharien from the next-door Christian Fellowship Hospital came to participate in the work camp. At one point during that day it started to drizzle. Most of us took cover, but Tharien continued working, saying, "It's only water. It will dry. Let's get the job done!" College students from many parts of Tamil Nadu were part of the work camp. Also, a student from Mysore and two students from Allahabad in North India joined the work camp. The boys from Allahabad were good at sports, but they took a ribbing from the Tamilians for speaking in Hindi. Sometimes I served as an interpreter for them: the Allahabad boys would tell me in English what they wanted to say, and I would translate it into Tamil for the Tamil-only speakers.

BASKERAN

R. Trinity Baskeran was a student pastor when I first met him; he was about four years younger than me. He had practically completed his undergraduate degree at American College in Madurai. Between June or July 1958 and May 1959, he served our Diocese as a volunteer student pastor/catechist in the Kallimandaiyam area.

I first met Baskeran in Kallimandaiyam in August 1958 when I started to come there pretty often from Vatalagundu to oversee the enhancement of the community center building where my family and I were to live. This involved building a wall surrounding the courtyard to give us some privacy and extending the bathroom to include a bathing area.

Baskeran and I really hit it off. He had the endearing quality of showing respect for his listeners and, at the same time, demonstrating that he felt totally equal to them. So he would speak the same to a Dalit person as to a high-caste person. He's always had such an easy way about him, and people respected him and liked being with him. He was fun to be around, and he and I shared many jokes.

We visited several villages together where there was a Christian congregation. Baskeran would lead the group in prayer and speak to them about the faith, while I might explore the possibilities of starting a loan society in their village. Initially, we traveled by bicycle, and then after September we made our visits using Keithahn's jeep while he was on furlough. We used to have meals together before my family and I moved to Kallimandaiyam. We were usually hungry so even the food in the one little restaurant in the village (in a thatched-roof building) tasted good.

Finally, in May 1959 I had to bid adieu to him, as he had to finish his education. I really missed him; we were like brothers.

Baskeran completed his undergraduate degree from American College and then entered Bishop's College in Calcutta (now *Kolkata*) for his theological studies. After completing seminary and ordination, he was called by the Madras Diocese of the CSI to serve as Presbyter at several pastorates in turn, starting with St. Thomas Garrison Church, St. Thomas Mount, Madras (*Chennai*). Other pastorates he served included *Tambaram* just south of Chennai and St. George's Cathedral in Chennai itself during 1984–85. During 1972–74, he did graduate work at Princeton Theological Seminary in the U.S., where he received his Masters in Theology. We were very fortunate in that we were able to see him a couple of times when he was there, as we were living quite close to Princeton in New Jersey.

Later, in 1988, Baskeran was elected as Bishop of the new Diocese of *Vellore*. The original Diocese of Madras (now Diocese of Chennai) had been bifurcated into a western portion (Vellore) while the eastern part remained the Diocese of Chennai. Baskeran stepped down from the bishopric eleven years later and is now retired and living with his son Alex in *Katpadi*, near Vellore, his wife Ethyl having passed away.

Jeremy and I visited him and his family in March 1984 when we made a brief visit to India. We met his wife Ethyl and his young sons, Alex and Chris. Baskeran was serving as pastor of the Tambaram pastorate at the time. When Hendrik and I paid him a visit in 1991, he was Bishop, and he and Ethyl were living in the Bishop's house in Vellore. And in March 2011, Skyler and I were hosted by him and his son Alex in Katpadi, and Baskeran showed us some of the rural development projects in the area. Chris was working in Chennai and was ill, so we didn't get to see him. Chris recently helped me by providing information about his father for the writing of this book.

Skyler, Baskeran and me March 2011

Baskeran has never deviated from his kind, humble, easy-going way of interacting with all people, as he loved and served our Lord.

HEALTH FOIBLES

During the last year in India (1960–61), I was bothered by stomach/intestinal ills. The doctors suspected amoebic dysentery, but stool tests did not positively confirm this. They also considered the possibility of ulcers. In that connection, I was given several tests, including 'barium swallow,' a series of X-rays during which you swallow a white liquid containing barium that coats your digestive tract and makes an ulcer more visible. These were not conclusive either. But to be conservative, they decided to assume that I was afflicted with amoebic hepatitis, and hence I might be experiencing liver damage.

In February 1961, I wrote to my parents:

> I still have my liver troubles with me. In October, I took a series of Nivembin tablets, with three days of Emetine injections. Then in November and December, I took a longer series of treatments with Viodochlor tablets. I went to see the doctor the third of this month again. He has put me on Nivembin tablets again (one after every meal for the first week of every month) for three to four months. Nivembin is supposed to be systemic in its action and also acts on the alimentary canal (like Entero-Vioform). He says that with this amoebic hepatitis, we are fighting a kind of cold war or war of co-existence. He thought my liver's size had gone down some since November. He wants me to take plenty of Vitamin B and have very balanced meals. I do feel better than in October and November. The pain kind of comes and goes. Some days I feel really good. And other days the pain is there and I get tired out very easily. I find if I eat rather moderate-sized meals with plenty of protein and vitamins, and don't go too speedy in my work, and get plenty of rest, then I get along quite well. But the pain and the tiredness do come fairly frequently.

I'm not saying all this to get everybody's sympathy (not that I abhor sympathy!), but so that Dad might have some more clues in the search I understand he was making about this disease. Recently I consulted Dr. Mary Cherian in the Oddanchatram Christian Fellowship Hospital (she delivered Jeremy!) about my ailment, and she suspects that it may have something to do with my digestive system. She thinks I might have dyspepsia or a small ulcer just starting, which didn't show up in the barium x-ray test. So she is giving me some medicine to take for this trouble for the next two weeks. Along with this, she has cut out all grams (dhal and other beans similar to lentils) as well as wheat from my diet. She says some people do not tolerate the gluten in wheat well. At the end of these two weeks, if it appears that there is still some evidence of the amoebic trouble, she'll give me injections of Chloroquine. Her approach seems sensible to me. After three days of this diet, I feel quite chipper today and with a minimum of pain.

MY WORK

My work in the Kallimandaiyam area just sort of evolved. Sometimes a suggestion from the Bishop or another diocesan official would lead to one or more projects. Sometimes, a small delegation of Christian or Hindu landless Dalits would suddenly appear in our little courtyard. They would have walked two to five miles from their village to get to our house. They would voice what they felt their situations/needs were and asked if I might help them.

LOAN SOCIETIES

In most of these cases, they were asking for loans—loans to buy animals, such as goats or Water Buffalo cows, or loans for purchasing material or equipment for tanning leather, if they were leather-working Dalits. In one village, the loans went toward the expenses of starting the cultivation of nearby government lands. In response to these requests, I set up informal revolving loan societies in four villages: Kallimandaiyam, Mandavadi, Rottputhur, and Veriapoor, all within 10 miles of our village. The way it worked was that each Dalit group in the village would designate from their group who all would get loans initially. Whenever each individual paid off his/her loan, that money would become available to loan to someone else in the society. A couple of months after we gave the loans, we would have periodic meetings in each village to report how much each person had paid back to reduce his/her debt and how much was available to give out as another loan. The meetings usually included encouraging members who had not paid their installments to pay up.

On May 7, 1959, I wrote to my parents.

> You know the Kallimandaiyam cow-buying cooperative. I feel that money loaned to such groups is a good way to help them, since it should keep building up. For if we were to give to individuals instead of a group within a village, it would be much harder to collect the installments for the loans regularly. This way, they exert social pressure on each other, and it looks as if they are all going to pay up in time.

As it turned out, these programs worked in the sense that the recipients used the loans for their intended purposes. Water Buffalo cows and goats, depending on the village, were purchased and nurtured. Tanning materials were bought and used appropriately. But the installment payments of the loans faltered in all four villages. Not enough money was generated in most cases for members to start paying off their loans.

In the end, I had to give up on even trying to get the loans repaid, and the societies folded. I had other projects that were demanding my time. Clearly, I should have done more research on setting up and managing loan societies to help these poor people. I should have sought training earlier on how to make such loan societies or co-ops successful.

FOOD DISTRIBUTION

Tamil Nadu usually gets its monsoon rains (the 'northeast monsoon') from September through December. Still, these rains are not nearly as reliable as is the southwest monsoon that western India and northern India receive from June through August. In the fall of 1958, the rains failed in our village area. This resulted in a very poor harvest in January 1959 of *cholam* (sorghum) and other millets grown on unirrigated land. It was that harvest that the poor people needed to have enough food to eat in the spring and summer of 1959. There was very little of any grain left in their houses in the spring, and with work still relatively scarce, some of them had to go without eating for a whole day or two at a time. One day in May 1959, Dalits from one village in our area had to walk eight miles to dig up scrungy sweet potatoes left in some field from the previous harvest.

During 1959–60, I had an ongoing prayer to God to bring rain to my villages, particularly for the Dalits. At times it was urgent; I was upset with God. Why would he abandon the poor this way? I questioned him and my faith. I suppose it was foolish, but the situation was urgent, and I was being honest with him.

In December of 1958, I learned that I had been selected as the contact person in the Oddanchatram area to receive and distribute surplus foodstuffs from the U.S. government. This could help alleviate the growing hunger in my area due to the failure of the rains that year.

Public Law 480, the Agricultural Trade Development and Assistance Act of 1954 (P.L. 480), unified existing surplus-disposal methods and U.S. foreign policy goals. The Act recognized there was a chronic excess capacity of American agriculture and a dollar-shortage situation of many food-poor nations. Title II of the act authorized food grants for emergency famine relief programs abroad through foreign governments. In 1959, P.L. 480 was officially designated the 'Food for Peace' program.

Almost uniformly, the body responsible for distributing the foodstuffs, the Commodity Credit Corporation (CCC), chartered by the federal government in 1934, used non-profit voluntary organizations to carry out the distribution once the food arrived at the destination nation. In my case, the shipments of food came to the Oddanchatram train station under the auspices of Church World Service, the U.S. National Council of Churches' international relief agency.

Once my new position's authorization formalities were over, I began to receive the food supplies at the Oddanchatram train station. I arranged for their transport to a storage facility and then planned for their distribution to the neediest villages. Usually, I wouldn't know in advance just what kind of food I would be receiving. We did get a lot of cartons containing cans of non-fat milk powder. We would also receive many sacks of grain, mostly wheat and rice, but also corn. The village people had difficulty with the corn as that grain was foreign to South India. Occasionally I would get cans of cooking oil and less frequently large tins of cheese, even more foreign to the people than corn. I was so glad I had Keithahn's jeep to take the food to the villages. I would distribute the food mostly to the landless Dalits, Hindu and Christian.

If it were a small shipment that would fit in Keithahn's jeep, I would bring it home and store it temporarily on our veranda or in our guest room. Otherwise, I arranged for transport to a storage room via lorry or bullock cart. At one point, we had to store 40 or 60 cartons of milk powder in our guest room.

On May 7, 1959, I wrote my parents:

> We are having U.S. surplus milk powder distributed daily in Veriapoor. And we are increasing the number of villages in which the powdered milk is mixed and given out daily. Still, the people need something more solid as well. I have written Bishop Newbigin and the director of surplus supplies in India to see if I can use such foodstuffs, as the 100 bags of yellow corn that just arrived at the Oddanchatram rail station, for distribution in the villages. According to the present rule, such grain supplies are to be used only in institutions with kitchens attached. I have also just sent a letter to inquire about the price and availability of Indian multi-purpose food (made from peanut meal and Bengal gram flour).
>
> In cases of dire need like this, I don't worry whether or not to give the food for fear of making the poor more dependent because one just must give when someone is starving. How badly

we need all the help we can get. It may seem odd and wasteful to Americans that the government is buying and providing all this surplus food overseas. But, there are sure many grateful people out here who are delighted to have these foodstuffs when there is very little other way to survive.

In late May 1959, I received permission to use the yellow corn I'd received for general distribution to famine sufferers. So, for the next ten days, I kept myself busy loading the jeep with sacks of corn and taking them to the needy villagers, mostly Dalits. They would soak the corn and pound it into meal themselves. They were *really* grateful, despite not being familiar with the grain.

One day in May 1959, the father of a boy in the boarding school in Kallimandaiyam came to our pastor Rev. Packianathan. He told him of the needs of his village and cried. He was a Christian, not the dependent type, but a real self-respecting Christian. We gave him three sacks of corn for his little Christian settlement, and we asked that if he felt moved, to share some of it with his Hindu Dalit neighbors living about three-quarters of a mile away. The next day when he came to return the empty sacks, he showed me a list of his distribution, including the names of the Hindu neighbors he had shared the corn with.

Some of the Christian Dalits in our area tried to take advantage of their loyal standing in the church, thinking they were entitled to more wheat, corn, milk powder, or more help in assisting their village industries. I tried to dispel this misconception, and the response to this on the part of our Christians and Hindu leaders was positive. I told the Christians that the only special privileges they had were the promises and hope the Bible assures us of.

On Wednesday, August 12, 1959, I had to go to Palani to be a witness in the sub-magistrates court. A young teacher in Carol Weeber's street-boys' school had been caught selling a case of U.S. surplus milk powder. Under the advice of Dr. Tharien and Rev. Packianathan, I made a complaint against the boy to the police. This move was highly unpopular among many in the Christian community. Still, there had been several instances of this kind of misappropriation in our Diocese, and our authorities had not taken any meaningful action. We thought it was time to take action in the governmental courts. The boy freely admitted in the police station his act and his sorrow for having done it. But the father had hired a lawyer, and the boy was now pleading innocent. It was an unfortunate thing. But letting the court action take its ordinary course seemed to be the only thing to do.

In the summer of 1959, without warning, I received a very large shipment of milk powder. There were 200 cardboard cases containing large cans of the powder. By that time, Jane had vetoed storing any surplus foodstuffs in our guest room, even though she had allowed it a couple of months earlier. So I was desperate to find someplace to keep the new shipment. After inquiring with people in Oddanchatram, I found a gentleman, Shanmugam, who had space in a warehouse he owned in town. When I approached him he was happy to accommodate me. So I arranged for a bullock cart to take cartful after cartful of milk powder cases from the rail station to his warehouse. I inspected the cases after they had been placed in the warehouse. I just assumed the shipment would be safe there, even though there wasn't a lockable door in that section of the warehouse. I wasn't as wary as I later learned to be.

Within a week, I learned that someone had stolen every single case of milk powder. I immediately drove down to Oddanchatram and viewed the empty warehouse. I talked to Shanmugam, and he said he didn't have a clue who the thief or thieves were. Then I reported the robbery to the police chief in town. He duly recorded the complaint and said he would be investigating it. Though I made many subsequent visits to the police station in town, the police chief told me each time that there wasn't any progress on the case. And after several months of trying, I gave up on it. I have to believe that some of the cartons or cans of the milk powder could have been traced by the police, as many of the hotels (restaurants) in town and neighboring large villages were eager to buy the powder for a price under the actual cash value. I'm sure Shanmugam must have been at least aware of the theft and got some kind of kickback, or maybe he himself pulled the whole thing off. I reported the loss to my Church World Service contacts in India. It was a terrible mistake on my part due to my unbelievable naiveté and poor judgment, but nobody took me to court over it.

In December 1959, Mr. Veeramani, the local member of the Tamil Nadu Legislative Assembly, brought up some of my work on the floor of the Assembly. I knew who he was and had spoken to him very briefly on one occasion. He formally accused me of using milk powder to convert Dalits to Christianity. I heard of this rather informally, and the authorities never pursued it. In any case, I had two friends in the government Taluk office in Palani, who voiced support for me, as they knew that I was distributing the milk powder fairly with no strings attached. I felt that I was hardly instrumental in converting anybody. If I were, it would have been by the power of God, I hope, not milk powder!

VERIAPOOR

Veriapoor was a village about three miles from Oddanchatram but off the main Dindigul-Palani road. The Diocese had already placed a Bible Woman, Packiammal, in the village. She taught the Bible to the women among the leather-working Dalits. Also, she taught the village women to spin cotton for their own clothes, using the simple bamboo spinning machines popularized by Gandhi. I made many visits to this village and got to know the leaders of the Dalits, Christian and Hindu. I also became friends with the Village *Munsif* (headman of the village), Velusami Naidu.

Whenever I would come to the village for a meeting with the Dalits to discuss loan society issues, the need for a water well for their community, or the new tannery, Velusami would always call for me to come to see him. He called for me via the leader of the Christian Dalits, Yesudas. Once at his house, he would invite me to sit up on his veranda sometimes for an hour or more. Meanwhile, Yesudas would stand at a little distance from the veranda, arms respectfully folded. Almost always, Velusami would give me a South Indian 'tiffin' (a sweet followed by a savory dish and coffee) or at least a banana and coffee, and we would talk about any number of things, Hindu philosophy, etc., you name it. We would only occasionally talk about how I was trying to help "his" Dalit people. The Dalit community of the village liked me to be on good terms with their *Munsif*, as he and other prominent caste families in the village were the keys to the Dalit community's long-term security.

Velusami never threatened me or discouraged me from what I was doing; I'm sure he wanted to maintain our friendship to ensure that the Dalits didn't start to get 'uppity' with him. In other words, he wanted to make sure that he and other higher caste people in the village would still have their normal power over "their" Dalits. In May 1959, Velusami spent several days traveling with me by jeep to help distribute the U.S. surplus grains by introducing me to leaders in other nearby villages who would hopefully see to the fair distribution of the grains to their poor.

The Dalit part of Veriapoor village was across the road from the caste part of the village. Both Hindu and Christian Dalits lived there. A small church had been built earlier for the Christians; it was right next to the main road, actually on the caste side of the village.

In May of 1959, I went to Dindigul to buy good-quality bamboos, the raw material needed so the village carpenter could resume making spinning wheels again. Many people had been asking me for spinning wheels, but I could not buy the bamboo until I received a monetary gift from friends of my parents. The Veriapoor carpenter was very happy also, as he had been without work for a while. I learned from Packiammal that the Dalit women had a harder time learning how to spin well than the higher-caste women. The Dalits were indeed in a vicious circle.

When I first started work in Veriapoor, we decided to form a loan society to help the Dalits purchase good partially-tanned hides and the chemicals needed for good-quality tanning. They already had the required essential tools of the trade, including four-foot diameter lime-mud tanks required for the tanning process. The money loaned through the loan society increased the village's leather production to an extent, but then due to low loan repayments, the society folded.

The second project that occupied me in Veriapoor was siting and arranging for a new drinking-water well for the Dalits. They, and in fact, Dalit neighborhoods in any village, had to have their own drinking-water well. For it was believed by caste people that if Dalits were allowed to draw water from a well the caste people used for their drinking water, the well water would somehow become impure. So I brought in a recommended 'water diviner'[1], and he found a good spot to dig the new well, along the main road and about 300 feet east of the Dalit neighborhood.

I located a local contractor who took on the project via a bid to the Minor Irrigation Department[2] of the District. The well, when constructed, was a 12-foot-diameter dug well with a three-foot stone parapet wall. The

---

1. Also called 'Water Dowser' or 'Water Witch'. This was before I was initiated into the scientific and engineering explanation of the occurrence and flow of groundwater in aquifers at the University of California at Davis. But still there's a corner of my mind that believes that *some* people might actually have the ability to sense strong flows of underground water. My missionary friend Charles Heineman and Dr. Tharien had some ability to do it I believe. For a scientific discussion, see https://www.usgs.gov/special-topic/water-science-school/science/water-dowsing?qt-science_center_objects=0#qt-science_center_objects

2. Which handled applications for new drinking-water wells also

well extended about 40 feet into the igneous rock. The well was needed because the government did not insist that the Dalits be allowed to take water from the caste drinking-water well. So they provided money in their budget to build separate drinking-water wells for caste people and Dalits. Usually, it was the Dalits who needed the wells. Until they got their own drinking-water well, women from that neighborhood would have to go as far as a mile to bring home water. They got permission from a caste landowner to draw their drinking water from his irrigation well. As it happened, however, the new well was also needed by the new tannery, to which I turn now.

In early 1959, I started to contact officials with the Department of Industries and Commerce for the Madurai District to obtain a grant from them to improve the tannery prospects for Veriapoor. After several meetings with them, I learned one day that they had selected Veriapoor to be one of the villages where the District would set up a demonstration tannery. Soon thereafter, they organized a Veriapoor tannery society of which I became a member, including a few members of the Dalit community in the village. The plan was to build a modern tannery building next to the new well described above. The Board of Directors of the society would direct the management of the new tannery. A tannery specialist, an expert in modern tanning technology, would be selected to lead the enterprise to tan the raw hides to the finished products.

In May of that year, we had the first meeting of the Veriapoor tannery society Board of Directors. We believed at that time that the government would be starting to build the tannery building by the middle of June. But in early August, I had to go to Madurai to urge the appropriate government official to begin the tannery-building construction soon and the subsequent development of the tanning industry in Veriapoor. We were still waiting for the Secretary of the Board to direct the society and oversee the building of the tannery building. In mid-September, I paid a visit to Chinnamanoor to see the government tannery building there. Chinnamanoor was quite a distance away—up the Cumbum Valley in the foothills of the Palani Hills. The tannery building planned for Veriapoor was the same model as in Chinnamanoor, so I wanted to see the general layout and some details of the building.

Later in the fall, the bids were received by potential contractors, and Mr. Samsudeen, a local Muslim contractor, got the contract. He had built one of the new buildings of the Oddanchatram Christian Fellowship hospital and was well regarded as a capable and honest man. South India has a relatively small population of Muslims. There was very little animosity between Hindus and Muslims that I could detect, unlike in the north of the country[3]. A well-off Muslim in Tamil Nadu named Asiz had been a staunch supporter of the Indian Independence movement and later was active in supporting the schools and the philosophy of Gandhigram.

Samsudeen on left and Vaishnavite Hindu friend on right

The tannery building was finished in the late fall of 1959, and by the first of the next year, the tannery specialist, Ponnusami, had been selected and, as they say in India, had *joined duty* (reported for work). Unfortunately, although they produced fine-quality leather, the tannery provided work for only a handful of men from the Dalit community.

3. There has been overt hatred of Muslims in parts of the North exacerbated by the current administration of Prime Minister Modi. Neighborhoods in New Delhi that for generations were integrated between Hindus, who make up the vast majority of India's population, and Muslims, who compose less than 15 percent, are now tearing apart along religious lines.

Velusami Naidu on the right at entrance to new tannery building

Far more disheartening, when I returned to Veriapoor in 1969 for a visit during my second term in India, I found that the tannery had closed. The problem was they could not produce the leather for the low market prices that existed. The demand for the leather had fallen sharply. Neither the officials in the District Industries and Commerce nor I had anticipated what would happen as the villages in the area became more and more electrified. With the onset of available electric power, farmers were less and less inclined to use the traditional *kavalai* system and more prone to buy electric-powered pump sets to draw water out of their wells to irrigate their fields. The *kavalai* system had provided significantly more demand for leather in the village area than anything else, because of the need to regularly replace the leather 'tubes' involved in the system.

In February 1984, when Jeremy and I visited South India briefly, we came to Veriapoor while we were staying at Dr. Tharien's in Oddanchatram. Many of the Christians we knew were still there, including Yesudas, and they were glad to see us. Naturally, the headman Velusami Naidu asked for us to come and see him, which we did. The Christians had prepared a "little" program for us in the church, which even Velusami attended, though he was sitting up on the altar platform with us. They had prepared some delicious *Tyar satham* (plain yogurt and rice) for Jeremy and me. It was fun to be with them all, and the Christians were pleased that Velusami and I still hit it off so well.

VALASAI

In the middle of February 1960, I was asked by the Diocese to go to the village of *Valasai* near Madurai to oversee the rice harvest on the excellent rice-growing land owned by the Diocese, now 2.5 acres in size. This was the land that Raja Rao had goaded the Diocese to buy to help the Christian Dalits of the village. In 1960 it was being farmed on shares to the Dalits on a 50–50 harvest proceeds basis. There were then four separate plots cultivated by four of the Christian Dalit families. Rev. Devapragasam, the Diocese's rural director, met me in Madurai one morning, and we drove out in his car[1]. We found that the rice yields on the diocesan land were meager. Devapragasam and I decided that the current share system did not encourage our Christians to use the best farming practices. So we decided to levy a specified number of rice bags per plot, to be paid as rent at harvest time for each parcel of land. Then anything above that would belong to the lessees.

---

1. A gift from Sherwood Eddy, a former missionary in the American Madura Mission, who years earlier had occupied the entire bungalow where we lived in Vatalagundu during 1957-1958.

NAVAKANI

In early 1959, I started to get many requests for new drinking-water wells or proposals to deepen existing ones to improve their supply. This led to my contacting government officers in the Palani taluk office and at the Madurai District level to see what available government programs might be available to pay for the wells. On a few occasions, I was able to take by jeep a government supervisor with his assistant and one or two well-construction contractors to different villages. They would study each proposed well site or measure the existing well, as the case might be. Several days or weeks later, the Minor Irrigation office[1] in Palani would ready the bids for the contractors to pick up.

They let the contracts strictly based on set government unit rates for each aspect of the work. Thus, partially due to my efforts, several wells were built or deepened in my village area. But no contractor came forward to construct a new drinking-water well for the Christian Dalits in Navakani, a village six miles east of Kallimandaiyam. So I stepped up and took the government contract for it.

Each village that I worked in was distinctive, not only because of the land's topography or the way the houses looked. Each village had a personality of its own. Villages displayed different cultures from others because of their distinct mix of castes, the village headmen/accountants' leadership traits, or the personalities and intelligence of the people making up the Dalit community.

In the case of Navakani, most of the caste people belonged to the Naicker caste. There was a small temple with a thatched roof in the village where the Naickers worshiped their idol. I was told that because the deity was in such a humble-appearing temple, the Naickers believed they could

---

1. The Minor Irrigation department took care of drinking-water well requests.

not build for themselves homes that exceeded their temple's appearance. Thus, all the Naicker houses in the village had only thatched roofs and mud walls, regardless of the wealth of the owner.

There was no village leader I could interact with in Navakani like Velusami Naidu in Veriapoor. In fact, in the many days I visited Navakani, not one of the Naicker caste people spoke to me. They kept their distance. I believe they looked on me as an intruder and a possible troublemaker. They didn't want the Dalits now Christians to advance at all. The only person I talked to besides the Christians was a Hindu Gounder, Murugaswami, a farmer residing in the village. We referred to him as the 'Friendly Gounder.'

But what was truly distinctive about Navakani were the young Christian Dalit men. They had a remarkable intelligence, and a sense of dedication and eagerness to improve their lives. Most every time I visited the village, I would speak with at least two of them, Mangalados and Sargunam.

Initially, I got ahold of a water diviner who spotted a good site for the new well about 100 yards north of the village. I found a reliable crew of well diggers to sub-contract to me to do the well digging. The men did the digging, and the women carried the soil on their heads out of the well in washpan-like shallow open containers. When the diggers reached crystalline bedrock about 12 feet down, they had to 'drill' holes in the rock by pounding on a straight crowbar and then set explosive charges in the holes. Naturally, the crew would vacate the well in advance of setting off the explosive. After each explosive event, they would get into the well again, and the crew would carry the broken pieces of rock out of the well. Finally, as we neared 45 feet in depth, the water started coming into the well at a reasonably good pace. We decided to stop there, and I brought in two stonemasons to build the parapet wall up to about three feet above ground.

During February through May 1959, I spent many days in Navakani as the contractor supervising the well digging and the parapet wall construction. In some ways it was pretty boring. But on several days, Murugaswami, the 'Friendly Gounder,' would come and sit with me. He would comment on what he believed was the ridiculous nature of the beliefs of the Naickers in the village. He ridiculed them. And he disparaged how the Naickers wanted to obstruct any sign of improvement in the lives of the Christians

Murugaswami was all for the work I was doing to help the Christians in the village. During Holy Week of the following year, a Good Friday/Easter pageant was presented by the Christian community of Pasumalai, a Madurai suburb. It was a very big affair, one eagerly anticipated by Christians of the Diocese. One day the week before the pageant, I went to Navakani and invited Murugaswami to accompany me when I attended the pageant one day. He readily agreed, which pleased and surprised me. The two of us set off one early afternoon in Holy Week on my motorcycle to go to Pasumalai, a distance of 65 miles. We enjoyed the evening program and then came home late that night. I never heard from him later about that experience and how it may have affected him. At a minimum, I hoped that it would have made him look kindly on the Christian faith.

Sometime in May 1959, the stonemasons completed the parapet wall for the well. By the middle of September, I got paid for the well construction at the Madurai Collector's office in Dindigul. But I wound up losing Rs 400 (about $90 then) because they allowed lower rates for deepening the well in rock than I understood initially; also, they didn't pay me for some of the masonry work for the well. They were unable to raise the estimate they had set initially.

The Christian Dalits had been asking if I could provide them with bathing rooms close to the well. So in January and February, I had them built using the same masons I used for the well's parapet wall.

In February 1960, I wrote to my Dad as he had given me some of the money to build the bathing rooms:

> Dad, I have finished the bathing rooms at Navakani. I guarantee their strength. Thank you so much. The Christian Dalits are pleased, especially the women who can now bathe anytime during the day, without having to wait for pitch dark evenings. There are two bathing rooms (not far from the new well) with a concrete holding tank in each room. The water can be poured into the tanks by pouring it into a sink-like feature on the outside of each room, which connects to the inside tank through a small diameter pipe through the wall. This will reduce the breakage of their mud pots, which would often happen if they had to take the pots full of water inside the rooms and then pour water into the tanks. The Christians contributed free labor for the bathing building. If they can learn to keep the rooms clean, I'm sure it will add to their overall cleanliness and sense of self-respect. They are keeping the concrete wet for 20 days, so it cures properly. After that, we will have a dedication for the building.

Many years later, when my sons and I returned to India in turn for visits, we visited Navakani. The first time was in early 1984 when I took Jeremy with me. That was the year when Dick Keithahn would die in December, but he seemed relatively hale and healthy then, so he accompanied us to the village. Dick was in retirement and lived in a small house on the Oddanchatram Christian Fellowship hospital's campus.

The Christians in Navakani knew we were coming, and they had prepared a big welcome party, complete with music, dance, and speeches, and of course, they garlanded the three of us. They had set up a platform on which we were required to sit during the program. After the program, I spoke with two of the young Christian men, Mangalados and Sargunam. They showed me their new homes they had built for their young families and described how several of them had gotten jobs with the government electricity department. Their eyes shown with pride. And, the congregation had built a new church on another side of the village. It was much more robust and quite beautiful compared to the old one, which they had allowed to still stand in its old location in the Dalit part of the village. And I was pleased to be able to greet my old friend Murugaswami.

Murugaswami Gounder on right during Jeremy's and my visit in 1984

In February 2011, when Skyler and I returned to India for a visit, we visited Kallimandaiyam late one afternoon. We found that a CSI pastor and his family now occupied our old house (community center). We found Rev. Thangaiyah at home with his family, and we introduced ourselves to them, and they hosted us briefly. It was late, but I wanted to see the congregations in Mandavadi and Navakani. The taxi driver who had brought us from Palani turned out to be a Christian and was happy to drive the pastor, Skyler, and me to both villages even though the light was waning.

When we got to Navakani, no one was expecting us. But many of the Christians quickly gathered at the church, where they greeted us. I had brief discussions with Mangalados and Sargunam. They must have been about 18 or 19 years old and I about 29 when I worked in their village. So they must have been 70 or so at the time of our visit. They looked well and greeted us happily.

Rev. Thangaiyah, Mangalados, and me in Navakani church in 2011

ANDERSONPATTI

Andersonpatti is kind of a strange name for a little hamlet about nine miles from Oddanchatram. It's about a half-mile closer to Oddanchatram than the town of Kannivadi on the road to Vatalagundu. A former missionary named Anderson helped to establish the village; *patti* is a Tamil postfix meaning 'place.' Anderson had a hand in the conversion of Dalits who had been living in Kannivadi. He purchased about 3.5 acres of land half a mile from Kannivadi, and he helped settle the converted Christians there. At the time I started the project at Andersonpatti, about 100 Christians were living there. Samuel was the community leader. He had received training as a lay catechist to lead services in their little church building when the pastor from Oddanchatram was preaching elsewhere.

In January 1960, a diocesan official suggested that I visit Andersonpatti to see if the three acres of the diocesan land could be developed to benefit the congregants there. I found that there were currently nine well-yielding tamarind trees and a drinking-water well on the far side of the property. Tamarind trees yield large brown leguminous pods containing a sweet, tangy pulp used in Indian cuisine, as are the trees' tender young leaves. Also, tamarind trees make first-class smokeless firewood for kitchens, so they fetch a good price. Every year or two the fruit (pods) had been auctioned off to the benefit of the Diocese.

My evaluation of the soil and groundwater availability for irrigation, as determined by a brief test of the existing drinking-water well, indicated that the three acres could be beneficially converted to rice paddy cultivation plots. The existing drinking-water well would have to be widened and deepened to maximize its yield potential for irrigating the proposed rice paddy fields. When I presented my proposal to the Diocese, they agreed to fund the project. The plan was to divide the land into four plots and have the landless Christians in the village till them in rotation.

Because I was starting to come to Andersonpatti pretty often and it was 20 miles from Kallimandaiyam, I applied to the UCBWM for money to buy a motorcycle, so I would be able to come home every night. The money came, and I bought a Royal Enfield with a 150cc engine. It was very helpful to me.

Someone in the diocesan Treasurer's office did some kind of cost-benefit analysis to demonstrate that the annual or biennial cash flow due to selling the Tamarind pods would be more than offset by the potential income from rice cultivation of the three acres. So the first work we undertook was cutting down and removing the tamarind trees, which I had mixed emotions about.

We started clearing the land of tamarind trees in late March 1960. And by sometime in late April, I had the wood all sold as firewood. It was a bit tricky getting it sold, however. I had to apply for two permits to allow us to transport it; otherwise, a Forestry Department man would stop the truck, demand to see a permit, and the truck would have to sit there for 4 or 5 days until the permit[1] was obtained. I had to go up to Kodai one day to get the two permits because that's where the government Forest Range Office was. We sold off the first six trees out of the nine in an auction.

A little later, we had an auction for the last three trees, but the auction was fixed against us. The highest bid for the three was only Rs. 270[2] ($60 then) and then the bidding stopped. Sensing the situation, I decided that since it wasn't a government-registered auction, I would stop the auction. Two days later, two people asked us privately and very eagerly to let them have the three trees for Rs. 425 ($95 then)! But we had already decided to have the cutting and felling of the trees done on our own. The woodcutter encouraged us in this. A few days later, one of the men who had offered us Rs. 425 met the woodcutter and said, "Because you encouraged their cutting up of the trees on their own, I have lost 200 rupees profit. I'll kill you. You'll see."

The man who did the threatening was a wealthy man in his village, a buddy of the village accountant,[3] and belonged to one of the 'thief' castes, quite possibly a Kallar. Being encouraged by the woodcutter and our local Christians, I wrote a strong letter to him in Tamil. I hoped it was a good mixture of persuasiveness and firmness. I talked with a commission agent and he offered Rs 35 ($7.80 then) per ton for the wood, but I thought we could get Rs 40, which meant I had to go to Madurai to make my own

---

1. The permit would certify that the wood came from private land and not government forest land.
2. 'Rs' refers to Indian rupees.
3. Often the leading man in a village

arrangements for the sale. In any case, the proceeds all went for developing the land in Andersonpatti.

By April 30th, we had completed the work, and the trees including trunks and roots had been removed. The next step was to grade the land into terraces because the land rose from the well up to the community's houses.

At about the same time, I contracted with a man who had a well-digging crew. The existing well had to be widened and deepened. In this case, we didn't hit any crystalline rock, but it was all calcareous soil to the bottom, about 35 feet below ground, moderately hard at some depths. So no explosives were required, just the men at the bottom of the well removing the hard soil with pickaxes and *manvattis* (short-handled mattocks). As with the Navakani well, the women laborers carried the chunks of calcareous soil out of the well on their heads, in wash-pan-like shallow open containers. As they continued the deepening, the diggers constructed steps on one side of the well for the workers to get in and out of the well. The photo shown here gives you an idea about the work being done in the well. It shows a *kavalai* arrangement for removing water from the well as digging continued.

Kavalai **system used in Andersonpatti well in 1960**

As the well deepening continued, I realized that the well's flow was significantly greater than what the *kavali* system could keep up with. So we stopped the well work for a few months. Further well deepening had to wait until we obtained funds to rent a diesel-powered portable pump set.

In April 1960, I let out a contract to construct the retaining wall and pump house for the well. I got a loan from the Block Development office (government) five miles from Andersonpatti to buy an electric pump set for the well. It was payable in ten annual installments. Also, I applied for an electricity line for the pump set. And we obtained the use of a bulldozer through the Block Development government officer to grade the land into terraces.

In January 1961, the Diocese gave us approval to rent a 10 HP diesel-powered pump set from an equipment store in Madurai. I believed it was powerful enough to keep up with the well flow until we had sufficiently lowered the water level in the well. I located a lorry service to deliver the pump set to Andersonpatti. We kept the pump set for two weeks, during which the well-digging crew resumed work and deepened the well a few more feet. In mid-February, I had to send the pump set back to Madurai because we couldn't afford to rent it for any more days. But I was confident about the well, as the underground spring had been proven to be strong. Even after pumping with the pump set every day from 6 AM until 5 PM, the water level would reach a low point below which it couldn't be pumped down any further.

We had to leave India to go on furlough in April 1961. So I was forced to leave the Andersonpatti project before the permanent pump set was installed in the pump house and before cultivation began. It was sad to leave Samuel and the other Christians of the village, particularly since I had not been able to put off our furlough by a few months to have seen the end of the project and the beginning of rice cultivation on the land.

In February 2011, when Skyler and I returned to India for a visit, we visited Andersonpatti on our way from Palani to Kodai. The small farm I had worked on had changed amazingly. The irrigation well was still operating, and the pump house had engraved on it the year '1960'. But the whole property appeared to be luxuriantly green with the green rice paddy fields and many coconut and banana trees, each plot full of young rice plants. Samuel, the congregant leader of the Christians in the village, took us through the fields. He told us that at some point, the land had been sold by the Diocese to a woman who was related to a member of the Andersonpatti congregation. So at least the Diocese got some income out of it, and the land was being used productively. However, it was unclear how any of this actually helped the landless Christian Dalits of the village.

Samuel, congregant leader, and me showing banana & coconut trees and rice paddy field in Andersonpatti in 2011

CLINICS

I had some responsibility for three CSI clinics, or health centers, in our village area: one in Mandavadi two miles south, one in Poruloor six miles west, and one in Veriapoor 12 miles to the south. Naomi, a midwife with general nursing training, stayed at the clinic in Mandavadi, so she was available 24/7. Philip and his wife were from Kerala, just west of Tamil Nadu, and they started out staffing a small clinic in Poruloor. She was a midwife and her husband was a medicinal compounder (pharmacist) with some general nursing training. They worked for several months in the clinic in Poruloor, then a larger clinic was established by the CSI in Veriapoor, and Philip and his wife were transferred there. Philip and his wife also had training in public health and in leprosy treatment and the rehabilitation of leprosy patients. A combination of the Oddanchatram Christian Fellowship and the Madurai-Ramnad Diocese of the CSI supported all three clinics.

In September 1959, I wrote to my parents and parents-in-law:

> I have a thorn in the side to share with you. In addition to the many other needs for the work here, a new need has come up. If you know any church group, medical group, or any other group of people who might like to support a regular project, here is one waiting for support. With the help of the Oddanchatram Fellowship, we have started a midwifery and general clinic in the village of Veriapoor. The Fellowship is supplying medicine, equipment, and meeting initial costs. We hope to make it as self-supporting as possible through local support. But now, at least, we'll need to pay the monthly salaries for the husband-wife team there. It will be about Rs. 140 a month total for both of them. So, $30.00 is needed monthly. The wife is a trained midwife and the husband is a trained medicine compounder, and he also has had

training in public health as well as in leprosy treatment and the rehabilitation of leprosy patients.

In November of that year, I wrote my parents:

> Thank you so much for all your bold, untiring, and fruit-yielding efforts for the work here. But rather than say 'work,' which is so impersonal, I would rather say 'for the poor people here.' The amount you sent for Philip and his wife was received, and it was paid to them for the month of October. Now we have received the check from Mary Fairbanks, and that will go through in a few days, so that will take care of their salary for November. Since you have the equivalent of several months' salaries accumulated, wouldn't it be easier for you to send it in a lump to me? I can bank it and give it out monthly. That will be no trouble for me. I am more than grateful for your efforts, especially when I know that canvassing for money even for the best purposes is not pleasant. I am thankful to the kind friends who have given gifts for the work through you.

Once in August 1959, when I was in Madurai, I went to see the district medical officer about the possibility of government support if we were to develop a program of family planning in our area. He didn't understand my English or Tamil very well. So I sent off a detailed letter to him describing the program and our needs. I never got any response from him.

BUSY DAYS

The following paragraphs describe the kind of busy days I had as I tried to live up to my work responsibilities. They are taken from letters I sent at the time to my parents and parents-in-law:

> 8/5/59: Next week will be busy for me. Tomorrow I visit the Street Boys' school in the morning. At 3 PM we have the managing committee for the Mandavadi health center. That night we start a loan society at Mandavadi to give small loans to enable some Dalits to cultivate government lands (*Puramboke*) held in common. Tuesday morning early, I start for Dindigul, and on the way I deliver wheat bags to needy villages. In Dindigul, I will see the government supervisor in charge of minor irrigation, which also includes drinking water wells. I need to arrange a day when he can come to inspect my new well in Navakani to check its measurements so I can get some money for building two bathing rooms near the well. At 11 am, the North local council rural work committee will meet in Dindigul. There we will discuss the five-year plan that I have proposed for this area. This is the plan that will be considered by Mr. Mook and Mr. Peters. In this plan, there are four points: Village industries (incl. spinning, weaving, tanning, etc.); Settling Dalits on government-owned common land, *Puramboke*, in agricultural colonies; Revolving loan societies; and, Family planning (in connection with general midwifery and out-patient clinics). Then I'll have the jeep given a badly-needed grease and oil change job and then head back home.

> 8/5/59: Thursday and Friday, I'll probably be busy with wheat distribution and well siting. On Saturday I have to be back in Madurai to attend Dr. Riggs's Preventive Health Committee.

Monday I'll have a document to sign since I am one of the attorneys for the American Board in the Madurai area. On Tuesday the 11th there is a meeting of the Industrial and Rural standing committee I have to attend. In all this, the difficulty is maintaining one's family and prayer life, including a sense of the spiritual dimension in all things.

8/5/59: I've just finished my milk powder accounts. Another burden lifted. Pretty soon I'll be through my desk work and actually do some work in the villages again.

2/15/60: Next Friday, I meet Rev. Devapragasam at Dindigul, where he will introduce me to his friend, Mr. Nairayanapillai, who is in charge of the government Harijan Welfare department in our area. I hope this gentleman can help us quickly get some good land into Harijans' hands in our area. That evening I have to be in Madurai again to present the five-year rural development plans to the diocesan planning commission.

7/7/60: I've got a new responsibility. I have been chosen by the Tamil Nadu Christian Council Economic Life (TNCCEL) committee to supervise the leather-tanning extension work of the newly appointed worker for this depressed area, which includes the Kallimandaiyam area and connecting areas in two adjoining dioceses to the north. As yet, no diocese has agreed to accept the TNCCEL's committee's offer to give loans for tanning in two or three villages in each of these three dioceses. Immanuel Muthanandam (the young man's name) is to teach the best tanning methods to the Dalit groups in the selected villages. For the present, we're trying to occupy him with making surveys in prospective villages and scouting out marketing possibilities for the tanned hides.

FUNDING

Funding for my projects came from different sources. For the village loan societies, I have my mother to thank. She and Dad donated quite a bit of money themselves, and then mother elicited donations from many of her friends, for which I was very grateful. The taluk government in Palani paid me directly for taking the contract to dig the well at Navakani. Payment was based on receipts I received from the well diggers and the masons. The District government in Madurai paid for the new tannery building and associated equipment at Veriapoor. And at Andersonpatti, the Diocese bore the cost to convert the drinking-water well (and deepen it) to an irrigation well and to grade the three acres to form terraces for rice farming.

On February 12, 1961, I wrote to my parents:

> About money for our work, I sort have promised two things. Bold of me, eh? A simple leather tannery for about 400 dollars and a house for the school warden and his wife at Kallimandaiyam for 500 dollars. About the last item, there is practically no house available for any of the teachers in Kallimandaiyam. And we've decided that a couple should be in charge of the hostel instead of single teachers, which we had up until now and which resulted in several difficulties. We think that a dedicated couple can really provide a nice family atmosphere for the poor boys in the hostel. I have written to Park Church[1] over a month ago to see if they would like to help with this house project, but no word yet. I have set aside $100 that came recently (in November I think) from the Women's Fellowship of Park Church for this house. Probably Park Church itself will help with this. For the tannery we can get money from the National Christian Council

---

1. Park Congregational Church, now under the United Church of Christ, in Grand Rapids, Michigan, was sponsoring us in India.

(NCC) of India. But, they require that it has to be a loan. The people in Veriapoor have already taken out loans to do simple tanning. If they take out another loan for building the little tannery it would be rather a burden on them. I would like to build the whole thing for them, and then ask the villagers to pay back, say one-fourth of the cost as a loan. Mother, I enclose three letters I've written as thank-yous for gifts I've received for the Poruloor clinic—to Anne Lawrence, Mr. McVaugh, and Alice Pyle. There'll be more to come in my next letter.

IN CONCLUSION

A SNAPSHOT OF A DEVELOPING FAITH

In May of 1959, I wrote to Shauna, Jane's youngest sister, who, as a very young person, was wrestling with how and what to believe as a guide for her life. Here's what I wrote to her:

> It's hard to come up with a philosophy of life that works out for oneself and fits all aspects of life. Life seems to be many times such a hodge-podge of different things that it's hard to have a consistent philosophy of life that takes care of all the details and contradictions. Better to have faith in someone/something else. Someone who can guide one, even though sometimes the details will be unclear and have to be filled in by common sense and prayer. However much I stumble, and however much I am unworthy of God's care, I still feel that he wants me to hang on to him and his son Jesus. There is so much to learn about life as related to faith and morality. The Bible will help at this point. Although in some ways (because of our age of science, doubt, and liberalism) the Bible doesn't seem related to our lives very much. In reality, though, the Bible is really very closely connected to our major problems, especially the Gospels, Paul's letters, and Acts. People of this century think they are ever so much more advanced over the first-century people. But I don't believe it. Each individual person's temptations and problems are about the same. Jesus was dealing with ordinary people in simple but marvelous ways. The people in the early churches of Galatia and Corinth had to be dealt with much the same as modern Christians need to be dealt with by pastors today. So, Paul's words are real and meaningful. Our age likes to think in terms of having one's own philosophy. Better to accept God's philosophy (his will) and follow the Master he sent us. It's not

easy, nor is it always fun. It means giving up a part of ourselves that we probably like and may even think good. But God may not think so. This is where repentance comes in. As C.S. Lewis says in *Mere Christianity*, "Now, repentance is no fun at all."

LEAVING INDIA

As early as May 1960, a year before we were scheduled for furlough, Jane and I started talking alone and together with friends about the possibility that we might not return to India after the furlough. By the end of the year, we had decided we would definitely not be returning to India in 1962. When the Board's Secretary for India and Ceylon, Telfer Mook and his wife Jane, were visiting Madurai in February 1961, he wanted to meet with all the Madura Mission members together. So we were happy to go and meet with them and the other missionaries. We were able to discuss with Telfer our decision not to return to India after furlough.

We learned in September 1960 that we were booked to leave India on April 22, 1961, on a Lloyd Triestino ship leaving from Cochin, Kerala, a port city on the southwestern coast of India. So we had six months plus to prepare for our departure physically and emotionally.

A month or two before we left India in April 1961, we began finding ways to sell or give away our various furniture items. Early on in that process, there were only a few items that we hadn't promised to sell or give to somebody or other. But one day when I was away, Pandian Pillai, our local village accountant and headman, came to see us. Without even asking the price, he told Jane that we should put him down for all the remaining furniture that hadn't been already spoken for.

Why did we decide to leave India for good? Jane was unhappy, more unhappy than she appeared. There were things about being in India she absolutely hated. The two of us drew up a list of things she hated about India, and we added to it as more things occurred to her. And then we would discuss them to see if any of her issues could be resolved in a second term. There were about 10 or 12 items on the list. I didn't feel I could work in India any longer if I didn't have her support and if she couldn't be tolerably happy there. As far as I could see, she saw little worth in most of the projects

I undertook. She was so pessimistic. So four months before we left, we had made up our minds not to return after furlough. But I could not predict at that time what that decision would mean for me in all its aspects.

Leaving India was hard. It was actually gut-wrenching for me. The closer the date of departure came the less well I was able to sleep. Then the loud cinema came to Kallimandaiyam almost permanently during March and early April 1961. I would drive my motorcycle to the nearby village of Mandavadi at bedtimes, where I slept on a long bench on the veranda of the CSI clinic there. Then fierce anxiety (near panic attacks) set in. But I had to continue what I needed to do: tie up my work obligations, pack all the things we were taking home with us, and helping Jane with the children. I got everything done that was expected of me during the trip preparations, the voyage home and later; that's the way I was raised.

But the feeling of panic and deep loss continued to be with me for a few years while I was working for a doctoral degree at the University of California in Davis and as we were raising our kids there. Try as I have done many, many times, I've never been able to figure out why my response to leaving India was as acutely and overwhelmingly painful, threatening, and devastating. I know I felt very bad about not completely finishing the several projects I had undertaken in the village area.

I also felt really sad about wasting all the time and money the Board had invested in me—my learning Tamil and the travel in India they provided for me to see first-hand some of the excellent rural development work being done elsewhere in the country. The Board had spent a lot of money and helped me in so many ways. They were losing in truth the further services of a promising missionary and his wife. And I felt really bad about leaving the Dalits in our area because my work and I stood up for them, and few were the people who did. I really loved them. Also, I felt extremely uneasy about trying to start a new life in the U.S. India was where I felt truly comfortable and at ease, no matter the challenge or problem.

But life went on, Jane and I survived, and our kids seemed to flourish. I threw myself into my doctoral program at the university. And near the completion of my work for the degree, Jane indicated she would agree to go back to India for another term if it could be worked out. So we started talking to Telfer Mook, Secretary for India and Sri Lanka of the United Church Board for World Ministries[1] (UCBWM) about a second term.

---

1. The UCBWM replaced the American Board of Commissioners for Foreign Missions when the Congregational churches and the Evangelical and Reformed Church joined together as the United Church of Christ in 1957.

We went back to India in July 1967, and at the end of the four-year term in 1971, we left India, never to return except as tourists. Just months before we left for India the second time, we adopted an adorable baby girl, Damaris Ann Ranjitham[2], to add to our three wonderful boys. For our second term, the Board seconded me to the newly-created Indian non-profit Action for Food Production (AFPRO), for whom I worked as a Water and Soils Specialist. But the second term is for another story.

To be a missionary, as a few of us were fortunate to be in those early days, you had to believe in the impossible dream. I remember the bright eyes of the Christian Dalit youth of Navakani (for example, *Mangalados* and *Sargunam*) and how they were helped to believe in themselves. Maybe, just maybe, we gave them a sense of heightened self-respect and a glimpse of hope, so they could really believe in what they could do for themselves. And belonging to a Christian church gave them an identity they could be proud of, rather than feeling they were the least of the least. Now "higher-caste" Christians must give their Dalit Christian brothers and sisters the respect equal to what they give to Christians of their own caste. I pray their hearts will be so turned by the love of God.

How fortunate I was to have spent a few of my early years interacting with so many people of goodwill in India and seeing Dalit people gaining some ground in their efforts to raise themselves up. I give thanks to my Lord God, who has led me, forgiven me, strengthened me, and provided me with the sustenance I needed every step of my life to carry on, despite difficulties, missteps, and my sins. To him, be the glory.

---

2. Ranjitham was the name of one of our dear Indian women doctors, Joseph John's wife in Deenabandhupuram.

EPILOGUE

They say that hero-worship is bad for your soul and fails to acknowledge the hero's feet of clay. But, during my first five years in India and beyond, I more than admired and made friends with at least three people—one Indian, Raja Rao, one American, Ralph Richard Keithahn, and an Englishman, Lesslie Newbigin. I didn't worship them in any sense, but each one was an inspiration to me as a young missionary, and each taught me so much about India, the Christian faith, and the Christian church in South India. They were giants in my life then and in my memories now.

RAJA RAO

Raja Rao against background of Ramnad District landscape in 1957

EPILOGUE

Close-up of Raja Rao in 1957

Bishop Lesslie Newbigin introduced us to Y. D. Raja Rao in January 1957, after the Bishop's secretary had recommended him to Lesslie. Raja Rao was a Christian and had taught in the missionary language school many years before when it was in *Chennai* (Madras). Lesslie wanted Jane and me to have the best Tamil teacher as soon as we had finished with elementary Tamil instruction in the language school in Bangalore and had passed the first Tamil exam. It wasn't easy to locate Raja Rao as he didn't have his own place. Lesslie finally learned one day in January through his contacts as Bishop, where Raja Rao was currently staying in *Madurai*, and then an arrangement was made for us to meet him at the YMCA in town.

On the appointed morning, we drove to that neighborhood and approached the YMCA building. Raja Rao wasn't hard to spot. Dressed in saffron robes and with a long beard, he appeared as a true *sadhu* or ascetic. We found him to have a reasonably sharp tongue, but also a keen mind for one over the age of seventy—so little did I believe at that time that one in their seventies could have a keen mind! His kind, gentle face was indicative of his heart. In excellent Tamil, Lesslie told Raja Rao that he needed him to do him (Lesslie) a favor: moving with us to our new home in Vatalagundu to teach us Tamil to help us pass our second exam in Tamil by the end of the year. Raja Rao took to the idea very readily, in fact, more readily than anyone who knew him would have expected. But then after coffee, and the arrangements were made for his coming to us, and we were about to take our leave, Raja Rao remarked, "As soon as you find out I have a bad temper and I find out you are lazy in your studies, we should get along well." As it turned out, Raja Rao never showed his bad temper to us, and I at least was so enthusiastic about applying myself to Tamil that he never labeled me 'lazy.'

Although one could see that Raja Rao was not an ordinary Christian, he firmly believed in the church and Christ's work in it. He stayed in Madurai a lot and was often active in evangelistic work of his own variety. Raja Rao had large posters representing some stories from the Bible and would write on them Hindu philosophical verses that he believed the Bible story or biblical event fulfilled. With these, he would go to the Brahmin sections of the city and speak to those folk.

We felt so lucky to have Raja Rao as our *munshi* (teacher), as he was well known for his scholarly nature. He was an expert not only in Tamil and English but also in Sanskrit. His forebearers were Brahmins from Andhra Pradesh, the state immediately north of Tamil Nadu. 'Rao' is the caste name of Brahmins originating mostly in Andhra Pradesh. He was born into a Christian family, his father having converted from Hinduism when his father was in his thirties.

Under his father's teaching, Raja Rao, although a Christian, incorporated many of the Brahmin traditions into his life. In Hinduism, traditionally, there are four stages (*ashrams*) to a man's life: the period of youth, study, and discipline; the period of marriage and raising a family; the period of seclusion in a forest devoted to meditation and prayer; and finally the complete renunciation of the comforts of home to teach about God out in the world. This last stage is one of the *sunyasi*, and it is such a vow that Raja Rao took some time in the 1940s.

Raja Rao was the nearest thing to a wandering mendicant in the church. At age 72, he had no home, nor any room to call home. He stayed with people who loved him and admired him, each for a few days or weeks at a time. Every day he dressed in a saffron-colored cotton *jibba* (formal shirt) and a saffron cotton *dhoti*. A dhoti extends from the waist down to one's chappels (similar to sandals). With his long white beard and his tall, thin frame, he was an impressive figure. Raja Rao was a Christian version of a sunyasi, a Hindu ascetic who, as indicated above, has renounced the world. He had abandoned any claim to social standing but would teach anyone who looked up to him as a guru.

As summarized above, in classical Hindu thought, a sunyasi was the fourth ashram (stage) of a Hindu man's life, usually taken up after one had performed a householder's role, including being married and raising his children. Only in this case, Raja Rao never married. His father died when Raja Rao was in his teens. After that, as the oldest child in the family, he was forced by the family's circumstances to study in a teacher training school and begin teaching in a Christian school as the family's breadwinner. He continued in several teaching posts to support his mother and ensure his younger siblings were educated. Later he decided to devote his life to God as a sunyasi. So marriage was not in the cards for Raja Rao.

Raja Rao was quite well known in the Diocese of Madurai-Ramnad, either approvingly as a supporter of the poor or as an agitator complaining against the Diocesan leadership. He felt many of the church leaders were ignoring the plight of poor Christians in the villages, most of whom were *Dalits*, the lowest rung in the caste system. Before I met Raja Rao, I came upon copies of a few of the colored leaflets he had printed and disseminated in the area. In these, he spoke out against those officials and pastors of the church who seemed to care more about enhancing their power and feathering their own nest than about improving the lives of the poor Christians.

When I thought about it, it was a gesture of reconciliation by Bishop Newbigin to reach out to Raja Rao and ask for his help in tutoring us, when Raja Rao had spared no words in his criticism of some church leaders, including the Bishop. At the same time, it could've been a smart move in the hope that at least while Raja Rao was teaching us, he might not have as much free time to crank out his 'troublesome' leaflets.

Raja Rao was concerned about the large number of poor in the villages and how the poor Christians were unable to support their own village churches. A year or two earlier, the Diocese raised Rs. 8,000[1] because of his pestering them, which the Diocese used to buy an acre and a half of excellent rice-growing land in the village of *Valasai* near Madurai. He arranged for two poor Christian families to farm the land as if it were their own. However, he told me that the land alone was nothing unless the Diocese could provide funds for rental of oxen and plows and the purchase of seeds. Being penniless, these folk would otherwise have to give up the land they were now allowed to cultivate.

The beautiful thing about the land Raja Rao through the Diocese provided for the landless Christians in Valasai was that for a relatively small annual payment,[2] the fields came with a water supply adequate for irrigating rice at two crops a year. The water flows from the Periyar reservoir in

---

1. At that time, the exchange rate was about 4.5 rupees (Rs) to the U.S. dollar.
2. In the most recent reference I could find, the rate ranges from $70 to $350 per acre/year.

adjacent Kerala State, and the outflow from the reservoir is diverted through tunnels into the upper part of the catchment to the *Vaigai* River, which flows eastward in Tamil Nadu past Madurai and thence into Ramnad District, discharging ultimately into the Bay of Bengal.

Constructing the Periyar dam and the system of irrigation canals in Madurai District, completed in the late 1940s, was great for the farmers in that district, but, as it turned out, was more of a disaster for farmers to the east in Ramnad District. They often saw the river coming their way downriver as just a trickle. The flow was diminished, starting about 15 miles west of Madurai by the diversion of the water into irrigation canals. Even today, Ramnad farmers cannot depend on getting any useful amounts of water from the Vaigai but have to rely on large man-made ponds, known as 'tanks,' which catch and store uncertain quantities of rainwater to irrigate their crops.

It was a treat every day to have lessons with Raja Rao. Mostly we sat out on cane chairs on the broad veranda of the bungalow. He was a fountain of knowledge about all things interesting to me. First off, about Tamil, including all the words used by Tamilians borrowed from Sanskrit. Sometimes these words had been Tamilized in everyday usage by substituting Tamil-like phonemes for the Sanskrit sounds not found in pure Tamil.

My passing the third Tamil exam near the end of 1959 was made possible by Raja Rao's excellent tutoring. But I must say I learned far more from him than just Tamil about: South Indian culture, the caste system, Hinduism, English, Christianity, and political machinations in the Madurai-Ramnad Diocese of the Church of South India, for whom I worked. No other Tamil *munshi* would or could provide his/her students with the added gift I received from him of actually seeing into the real, though often undercover, happenings in the church and the society there.

He told me of rumored embezzlement/corruption by a few officials in the Diocese, but also of the sincere Christian work performed by pastors such as Rev. Thangaiya, a CSI pastor stationed in the northwest corner of the Diocese where our family would soon move to. I learned of the indiscretions of the wife of a local Tamilian pastor and a previous indiscretion between a male missionary in the Madura Mission and an Indian woman. Raja Rao relished being able to share with me all gossip-worthy happenings recent or past.

Raja Rao told me about a Christian family in Madurai. The head of the family, Chinniah Naidu, and his wife had a daughter and a son. Their daughter Dr. Chinniah was an excellent doctor in the mission hospital in Madurai, a lovely lady who also practiced privately. They sent her brother, Devaraj, to America to study in college. The boy fell in love with an American girl there and they married. Raja Rao told me that this prompted his parents to disown him, as he had married out of caste. Caste was that important even to Christians, especially considering that Naidu was a relatively high ("forward") caste.

Though of a high-caste background, Raja Rao usually came down on the side of Dalit[3] Christians in instances of conflicts among different communities (castes) in the church. Yes, caste was and is alive and well in the church, but not uniformly. But there's still very little intermarriage among different castes in the church. Raja Rao saw our Diocese as being essentially under the control of members of just one "forward caste," the Velalars, who held the positions of Bishop's Commissary (Rev. Paulraj Thomas), diocesan Treasurer (G. G. Joshua), the Dindigul Local Council chairmanship (Rev. Sam Devapragasam), and after Bishop Lesslie Newbigin resigned in 1959, the bishopric itself in Rev. George Devadass.

I know that when we were living in Vatalagundu, Dalit Christians in the CSI compound included the pastor of the Vatalagundu church, Rev. Ponnusami, and many of the teachers in the two schools. Raja Rao confirmed that they believed that the forward-caste Christians in the Diocese were disrespecting them and discriminating against them.

As an update to the caste-biased leadership of the Madurai-Ramnad Diocese, a story in *The Hindu*, the respected English-language newspaper in South India, described in its May 25, 2013 issue the selection of a new Bishop for the Diocese. Out of 13 candidates, a Dalit pastor, Rev. Baninga Washburn, emerged as the winner in the first two rounds of votes cast on December 20, 2012 in Madurai, while Rev. M. Joseph, a member of an intermediate caste, came in second. Five months later in May 2013 the Moderator of the CSI had still not officially announced Rev. Baninga as the winner, which was highly unusual. At that stage, several of the Dalit Christians in the Diocese, who have historically been silent about the prevailing prejudices, began to publicize the issue. They were saying that caste prejudices still existed in the church and that one's caste identity trumps the Christian faith. Nevertheless, several days after the article appeared in *The Hindu*, the CSI Synod selection committee met and, in their wisdom, decided that Rev. Baninga Washburn would not, after all, make a satisfactory Bishop despite his election victory in December, and chose Rev. M. Joseph for the position. Some would say that the bishopric election in December 2012 was stolen

---

3. Earlier Gandhi had named the Dalits, formerly 'untouchables', as *Harijans*, 'people of God'.

from the *Dalit* Christians of the Madurai-Ramnad Diocese. Dalit Christians are believed to make up at least 60 percent of all Christians in the Diocese.

Raja Rao never commented on my coming out to India as a missionary. He never praised me for volunteering my services to help the poor in our part of South India. That made sense, considering there were, and now are, more than enough Indians who know how to run the church and denominational colleges and how to utilize and create beneficial technology. But he made one personal comment about me one day in response to something we were talking about. "You must have had good parents," he said. But this was before he met my parents; they came to see us in 1958, soon after Skyler was born and after we had moved to our village, Kallimandaiyam.

Jane and I passed the second Tamil exam late in 1957, and I volunteered to take the third and last Tamil exam. So Raja Rao was thankfully destined to be in our life a little longer. After we moved to Kallimandaiyam in October 1958, there was no room for Raja Rao to live in our new home as we often had guests who wanted to see what we were up to. So for more than a year until my third exam in December 1959, we found a room for Raja Rao in the pastor's house in Oddanchatram, some nine miles south of us. I used to drive Keithahn's jeep down to Oddanchatram to get my daily Tamil lesson with him.

In addition to everything else required for the third Tamil exam, Raja Rao also guided me through the couplets I had to study, selected from the long classical Tamil poem *Tirukkural* by Thiruvalluvar. At the time it was written, about 300 BC, Tamil writers, greatly influenced by Buddhism, commonly wrote on ethics. The *Tirukkural* itself is a comprehensive manual of ethics, polity, and love, containing 1,330 couplets or *kurals* divided into chapters of ten couplets each. The first thirty-eight are on ethics, the next seventy on polity, and the remainder on love. I had to study just twenty of them. Each couplet of this work is very stingy with words in expressing wise admonitions and advice, and the words used are esoteric, rarely used in the ordinary language. But the *sound* of a Tamilian reading from the *Tirukkural* is beautiful to the ear. Here are a couple of examples translated into English[4]:

> Since goodness doth produce prosperity and joy in heaven,
> What greater wealth can any man desire?

> 'Tis true morality to be blameless in the heart.
> All else is empty show.

---

4. White, *The Wisdom of the Tamil People*, 15.

On the other side of learning a new language, Raja Rao gave me the essential skill of speaking Tamil colloquially, the way the language is actually spoken. As in, for example, "*Ayya, varuhirain*" ("Sir, I am coming to see you.") converts in ordinary speech to "*varaininga*," the suffix "*inga*" already implying you're talking to someone deserving respect. The other meaning for "*varaininga*" is just "Goodbye, Sir/Madam"!

Most missionaries I ran into learned to speak formal Tamil and stopped there, so they didn't have the enjoyment of speaking the language the way it was ordinarily spoken. Like most languages, I suppose, people figure out how to say the same thing but with special shortcuts to give the tongue a break. One time when I was returning on a bus from a church event out of town, I was dressed in a white *jibba* and white *dhoti*. The man sitting next to me on the bus took me to be a Brahmin and spoke to me in Tamil. He said that the way I was speaking Tamil colloquially, I sounded like someone from the city of Madras, now Chennai!

Here's what I wrote to my parents about my Tamil studies toward the end of 1959:

> 11/12/59: I am managing to study every day. Raja Rao is in good form. We are practically through with all the poetry and other literature and are concentrating on the oral part of the exam, which means conversation, newspaper reading and discussions, and sermons. Naturally I have to give the rest of my work a lick and a promise, but it will all be over in three weeks, and I hate to risk not passing the exam and then waste the Board's money that they are spending on Raja Rao's salary and for my travel to Bangalore to take the exam. I am taking the oral part in Bangalore and the written part in Madurai a week earlier.

> 12/22/59: My exam wasn't as hard as I feared. The oral examiners were real nice to me, and we had a nice time talking (in Tamil). They say I passed with distinction, but I haven't got the formal results yet. It is such a relief to be completely free of all Tamil exams! Now I can breathe free and begin picking up ordinary colloquial Tamil in earnest.

After I passed the third Tamil exam in December 1959, I sadly no longer needed Raja Rao's services. He went back to the Madurai area and stayed as before with friends and family. I missed not having my Tamil lessons with him, and in particular, I missed not having him near. I can't exactly remember the day when I said goodbye to him as we were preparing to return to America in the spring of 1961.

Happily, we returned to India in July 1967 (six of us, including our nine-month-old adopted daughter Damaris), but were stationed in New Delhi. My first trip to the south connected with my new duties under Action for Food Production led me to Madurai. The first order of business was searching out Raja Rao, who was in his eighties then. He was staying with one of his nieces and her family in a new housing development on the northwest side of Madurai. He looked exactly the same in his saffron jibba and dhoti. His niece and family invited me to stay overnight. Raja Rao and I had welcome discussions that evening, catching up with each other, including his telling me what was going on in the church and society since we had last seen each other.

It's a funny thing to remember about that overnight stay, but it was about my taking a bath the next morning using the water from the well in their backyard. The water was the hardest water I'd ever tried to wash or bathe in. The soap I was using was no match for the water; there was no soapy feel whatsoever to the water as I tried my best to shave and bathe. But then by way of compensation, as soon as I dressed, Raja Rao's niece treated me to one of my tastiest South Indian breakfasts.

A few months later, when I returned to Madurai again, I went to his niece's house, and she told me that Raja Rao had died the previous month. She also mentioned that one of his sisters, Lakshmi, had retired from the mission hospital and was living in the hospital staff quarters in the city. I went and sought Lakshmi out and finally found the small room she called home. She was at home and answered the door when I knocked. As soon as I saw her, and as I peered into her room, it was evident that she was living on the smallest possible retirement pension. Could Raja Rao's sister be living in this kind of poverty? I guess she might have felt grateful, though, that she was being allowed to live out her retirement in one of the hospital's staff living quarters. I told her how much her brother had meant to me and put money in her hand in honor of him. I don't remember how many rupees it was. I never saw her again. I loved Raja Rao and miss him even now.

KEITHAHN

Dick at age 61 at my parents' home in Detroit when he was on furlough in 1959

Dick Keithahn at age 60 at Gandhigram

The Divali lights were flickering when Dick Keithahn (Ralph Richard Keithahn) rose to speak at the evening meeting. He was an imposing figure, and he spoke deliberately and lovingly and with great confidence to the assembled villagers and Gandhian workers. He spoke of the way which Gandhi had pointed to, how all castes could work together in peace as brothers and sisters. I felt as if I was listening to a prophet. Did the others present feel that too? Or had they come to see a "reed shaken by the wind," or "a man clothed in soft raiment?"

What follows is the recounting of my experiences and perceptions of my friend Dick Keithahn, who lived and spoke prophetically to many of us in India.

When the Millses came on the scene in 1956, there was an exciting controversy going on between the CSI Bishop of the Madurai-Ramnad Diocese, Lesslie Newbigin, representing mainline ecumenical Christianity, and Ralph Richard Keithahn representing a kind of reconciliatory Christianity whose aim was to be open to Indians of all faiths and to be untainted by colonialism. I received issues of the *Guardian* and the *South India Churchman* for a few months just before we came out to India in 1956, and every issue or two would bring an article by Dick Keithahn or one by Bishop Newbigin, in which each would respond to the previous article by the other.

Keithahn's Christianity saw more to be gained for Christ by demonstrating complete respect for the cultural and religious background of Indian people rather than by denigrating their traditional religious beliefs and practices. Dick would write about the value of holding inter-faith prayer services among Hindus, Muslims, and Christians for peace and reconciliation, *and*, Lesslie would respond to one of Dick's articles saying that Christians should never participate in any worship service in which Jesus Christ was not the Lord of Lords. It was fascinating, especially knowing we would be working in the very same district where these two giants of Christianity were working. It is important to point out that Dick was in no way saying that Christians should give up their daily prayers to Jesus or forego their regular services in their churches.

In his memoir,[1] Dick describes some of his interactions with Bishop Lesslie Newbigin during the years 1947 to 1959. Initially, when Dick and his family came back to India in 1947 after she gained her independence, the newly-formed Church of South India accepted him as a Presbyter. But Lesslie didn't approve of Dick's theology and so Dick began to feel less and less accepted by the Diocese over the next several years. Finally, when he came back from furlough in 1959, Lesslie let it be known through his advisors that Dick could no longer administer the sacraments as a Presbyter. But later that year Lesslie resigned from the bishopric and Bishop George Devadass was consecrated as Bishop of the Madurai-Ramnad Diocese. After the consecration, Dick went to see Bishop Devadass to discuss the matter. Dick tells us in his memoir that the Bishop declared "I have no trouble with your theology." Soon after, the Diocesan personnel committee recognized Dick as a Presbyter and the UCBWM followed suit by recognizing him as an associate missionary with a special portfolio in the Madurai-Ramnad Diocese.

Dick mentioned in his memoir how kind and courteous Lesslie was to him, despite their major disagreements on Christian theology. Dick noted that when he would come to see the Bishop, Lesslie "would get up from his

---

1. Keithahn, *Pilgrimage in India*, 65–66.

desk and come and sit *with* me." And one time when Dick happened to meet Lesslie in Kodaikanal sometime in the early 1970s, Lesslie[2] "stopped his car, got out and shook hands [with me]." Dick continued, "One appreciates such Christian courtesy, especially when one knows that there is a good deal of difference in Christian outlook."

I can't remember precisely when I physically met Dick. Jane, Hendrik, and I arrived in Madurai in March 1956, and within a few days, we were sent to Kodaikanal to begin studying Tamil. We must have met Dick sometime before June when we left to study at the missionary language school in Bangalore. Dick's younger daughter Ruth had completed her course work at Kodaikanal School the year before and had spent time traveling around India for the next 12 months. In May 1956, she was preparing to leave India to begin college in the U.S. Dick had arranged to take her to Ceylon (Sri Lanka) before she left for the States. I remember talking to the two of them a few days before they left for Sri Lanka.

Ten months after our arrival in India, Dick took the three of us (Jane, Hendrik, and me) in his old jeep from Kodaikanal, over the mountain road through the tea estates to Munnar in Kerala. In that state, we visited several places along the southwestern coast of India. He introduced us to interesting friends, many of whom were Gandhian and who had been active in the Independence movement. Some were Christians living in ashrams there, who also closely identified with Gandhi's leadership in the independence movement. What was unusual about this trip by us four was that we didn't stop to visit a single *dorai* (white gentleman) or *doraisani* (white lady); we met and stayed only with Indians.

It was a trip we would probably never have experienced with any other missionary. We traveled and slept and ate just as did Keithahn and his Indian friends. We attended an all-India meeting of the Fellowship of Reconciliation, at which Dick spoke. Then we drove south, then east, then north into Tirunelveli District in Tamil Nadu, and thence along the Western Ghats (mountains) to the Cumbum valley. In Cumbum, we stayed the night with the Rev. Rajanayakam, the Church of South India (CSI) pastor at Cumbum, and his family. Imagine, the older missionary dorai and his new young missionary colleagues spending the night on the veranda of an Indian pastor's house! Not very common in any sense in 1956, and it would have been rather shocking in 1925 when Dick first came to India as an American Madura[3] Mission (AMM) missionary. I loved it.

2. Keithahn, *Pilgrimage in India*, 65.

3. Since Independence in 1947, the city and district is known as 'Madurai', its Tamil name, rather than Madura.

Dick's activities as a missionary and his style of ministry were well known in Christian circles in South India. And his activities and style were often the subjects of some debate. During the last half of 1956, Jane and I were studying Tamil in the missionary language school in Bangalore. One evening the language school students were invited over to Russell Chandran's home in the compound. Dr. Chandran was the Principal of the United Theological College, which was on the same compound as the language school. The evening had a relaxed and enjoyable atmosphere. The subject of missionaries' identifying with Indian people came up. And of course, in the next breath, someone mentioned Dick Keithahn. Russell made the point that while living simply may help missionaries identify with the people, it can lead to family conflicts, as seemed to be happening, he said, to Dick and his wife Mildred. I believe that Russell spoke for those well-educated and well-placed Indian Christians whose consciences may have been pricked by Dick and Mildred's voluntary poverty. I later learned that the disagreements and resulting separation of Dick and Mildred had nothing to do with their living simply, so Russell clearly misspoke.

Between 1947 and 1956, Dick had worked with Gandhian colleagues to help create and develop the educational institutions in Gandhigram[4], located near Dindigul. But a little before Jane, Hendrik, and I arrived in In India in 1956, Dick had decided to leave Gandhigram. As he was a member of the Madura Mission living in Madurai District, it was natural that he would work under the Madurai-Ramnad Diocese of the Church of South India (CSI). Sometime soon after the family and I went to live in Vatalagundu in late 1956, Dick was assigned by the Diocese to serve as Correspondent (Manager) for the Vatalagundu Basic Training School. Bishop Newbigin was the bishop of the Diocese at that time. One might ask, given the attitude of Bishop Newbigin toward Dick's theology and practices, how could Dick have been appointed as Correspondent to a CSI institution? Dick had a supporter in Lloyd Lorbeer, a soon-to-retire missionary who lived in Pasumalai and was the outgoing Correspondent of the training school.

Lloyd was another missionary with genuine dedication; he had a great love for the Indian people and endeared himself to many Indians by commonly riding his bike out to villages rather than coming in a mission car. He would put his bike on top of a bus in Madurai, ride the bus as far it went, and then cycle the rest of the way. Lloyd appreciated Dick's ministry and his

---

4. Gandhian Training Institute in Madurai District of Madras State which Dick helped to create in 1947. Gandhigram was founded on the principle of 'basic education,' the educational philosophy of Gandhi that emphasized educating village children so that they would be encouraged to stay in their own villages.

approach to mission. I suspect that it was on Lloyd's recommendation that Dick became the Correspondent at Vatalagundu.

The Vatalagundu Basic Training School gave two years of training to young men who had at least an eighth-grade education. The training enabled them to work as elementary-school teachers in basic education in village schools. This training school, although under Christian management, received grants from the government. The Correspondent was responsible to the Diocese for the school's proper operation, and he or she had final responsibility for the financial accounting. The headmaster of the school reported directly to the Correspondent.

Soon after we moved to Vatalagundu in December 1956, Dick made our bungalow his part-time headquarters. The CSI compound in which the bungalow was located included a basic training school, an elementary school up to the eighth standard, and the Vatalagundu CSI church. And along the western side of the compound, there was a row of simple homes, where the CSI pastor and the elementary-school and training-school teachers lived. The mission bungalow had been built a hundred years earlier by the Madura Mission. Sherwood Eddy and his family, under the AMM, lived in the bungalow way back in the first decade of the twentieth century; they occupied the entire house then.

Now it was a new age, and many people lived in the bungalow. The Headmaster of the Training School, Mr. Venkatasami, and his wife and two children lived in the eastern side of the bungalow. My family occupied the western side, and we had the use of the flat roof and one of the two upstairs bedrooms. In the central portion of the bungalow, some of the training-school boys slept, as did Dick when he visited the school. Dick made the bungalow his headquarters during these visits, sometimes several days at a time. He often ate with us, and the rest of the time when he was 'in station,' he ate with the training-school boys or with the Venkatasamis.

Dick had been a vegetarian since long before I knew him. He would eat eggs, but never meat, poultry, or fish. He had become a vegetarian because, similar to Albert Schweitzer and his 'reverence for life', he didn't want to take the life of an animal and because he didn't want to offend his vegetarian Hindu friends, including Gandhians. Another concern that led to his adopting vegetarianism was that he didn't want it to be prohibitively expensive for poor people to entertain him in their homes. Most non-vegetarian Indians feel they must serve meat to an honored guest.

Dick always read and had devotions by himself in the morning before breakfast. By the time I would be dressed and ready for breakfast, he would already be dressed and would have had his devotions. I can remember

Dick's taking his early afternoon naps in the room next to our office/living room. He always took a half-hour nap after his noon meal, seeming to sleep soundly, and then be up and begin the work of the afternoon. I think his napping was an excellent habit and discipline, especially in the hot season, for he was an early riser. (More than a half-hour's nap in the hot season would probably leave one drenched in sweat!) Many times he would use our bathroom to take his daily pour bath. I do believe he could bathe faster than anyone I've ever seen, for in no time, he would appear dressed, bright-eyed and bushy-tailed, and eager for breakfast or whatever he had on his schedule. It was at these times that his humor would be most evident, and he would gently rib us.

While Dick opposed mass conversions to the faith, he was deeply concerned about the condition of the poor Christian Dalits in the Oddan-chatram-Kallimandaiyam area who had already declared their faith in Jesus Christ. To begin with, they needed to be tutored in the basic elements of the Christian faith. The CSI pastor at Oddanchatram, Rev. Packianathan and Rev. Thangaiya before him, had the responsibility of nurturing these converts. But there were more than fifty such village congregations under their care! To supplement their work, Bishop Newbigin had wisely initiated a program of recruiting and training lay pastors at the village level. Dick applauded this program as far as it went. These catechists nurtured the new Christians in their own village and nearby villages. They were joined by a few 'Bible women' who had been similarly trained and who taught the Christian, and sometimes Hindu, women of the villages were they were stationed.

Dick established a fund with the help of his family to assist in building village churches mostly in the Oddanchatram-Kallimandaiyam area. The way I remember its working was that a village congregation would request that a church building be built in their village. If the Diocese approved, the congregation would pay for putting up the walls, usually of mud and lime, and money from the Keithahn fund was then used to put a roof on the structure, made of wooden beams, rafters and tile roofing. I believe that the money from Dick's fund went through the Diocese and from the Diocese to the local pastorate. I don't believe that Dick oversaw the church-building work, nor provided the money directly to the roofing contractor. In his memoir, Dick states that his program had been responsible for building six churches in the area.

Along with responsibilities at the Vatalagundu training school and the Kodaikanal Ashram Fellowship, Dick became active in the *Bhoodan* movement. '*Bhoodan*' means 'land gift' in Hindi. Vinoba Bhave, a disciple of Gandhiji, led this land-gift movement. Vinoba, referred to as Vinobaji by those who loved him and worked with him, would walk from village to village begging the landed to deed over a portion of their land to the landless. Usually Vinobaji did not walk alone, but was accompanied by followers, local villagers, and well-wishers. He would point out to landowners of a village that the average Indian family had five children. He would ask them to consider him to be their sixth child. So he would ask them to give him one-sixth of their land so that he could deed it over to the landless poor.

This movement became a part of the Sarvodaya movement, which was broader in purpose and intent than just begging for land and distributing it to the poor. The concept of Sarvodaya is roughly analogous to Jesus's words: "Truly I tell you, whatever you did not do for one of the least of these, you did not do for me." The word 'Sarvodaya' literally means 'the rising of all,' the idea being that not one person is left behind in helping a village to rise to a higher level of development. Contrast this idea with the 'trickle-down theory' that was in vogue among international development agencies for a time. Maybe it still is.

One thing that helped to give the land-gift portion of the Sarvodaya movement more momentum than it might otherwise have had was that Jayaprakash Narayan put his full political weight behind it. He had run several times for national office on the Socialist ticket and was highly thought of by members of the major parties. When he decided to back the movement, he gave up his political aspirations and worked mostly at the grass-roots level of the movement.

Vinobaji started begging for land in 1951 in villages in the now-existing state of Telangana in south-central India. By 1956 he had come into the south. Amazingly enough, acre upon acre and 100 acres upon 100 acres began to be donated. Sometimes though, farmers would deed over the poorest portion of their land.

I was fortunate to meet Vinobaji one day in 1957 when I happened to be in the Kalupatti area of Madurai District. He was in the village he had walked to the previous day and was planning a meeting there in the evening to plead for land gifts for the landless of the village. I was able to have a personal interview with him for about 20 minutes that afternoon. I found him to be a rare soul, one to inspire anyone who sought God's will.

In some villages, a small revolution occurred when all or most of the landowners in a village decided to deed over land to the village, so that it could be cultivated in common by the village as a whole. If this happened, the village was called a *Gramdan* village ('village gift'), and there were several such villages in the Vatalagundu area.

The handing over of land to the landless was not without its problems, including the need for training of the landless farmers to manage a small farm and arranging for credit for purchasing the implements, seed, and fertilizer they would need. And, disputes about the land broke out in some of the same villages where compassion had been shown through the donation of land.

All this meant that after Vinobaji and his core followers moved on to another village area, someone had to stay in the *Bhoodan* or *Gramdan* village to help the villagers sort out their newly-found opportunities and problems. This is where Dick Keithahn and some of his colleagues in the Sarvodaya movement came in. There were many meetings with the villagers of each *Gramdan* village, many arrangements to be made with government banks for loans, and untold other details.

The *Bhoodan-Gramdan* movement no longer exists as a movement. It lasted about 23 years, 1951–74. During that period approximately 2.5 million acres had been given to the landless and 5,000 to 7,000 *Gramdans* had been established. Of those, approximately 3,900 villages were still under Gramdan law by 2011[5]. In most instances Gramdan law stipulated that the land could not be sold or kept as mortgage; it had to be cultivated and be managed by the Village *Sabha* (Association).

I think the *Bhoodan-Gramdan* movement stopped largely because it lacked a truly inspirational figure to replace Vinoba after he decided, before he died in 1982 at age 87, to take up other causes. One of the campaigns he took up in 1979 was a fast to achieve a ban on the slaughter of cows,[6] which are sacred to most Hindus. But according to Shah (2011), the movement failed largely because the forces opposed to the movement—the political and social elite including large landowners—proved stronger. These elite ridiculed Vinoba's *Bhoodan* and *Gramdan* claiming that all the land he had gathered was on paper or was of poor quality. But, according to Shah, the reality of the concept in the *Gramdan* villages touched the hearts of the people, who gave widespread support for it. According to Wikipedia[7], though the movement failed to sustain its early attraction, it made a long-term contribution to Indian society by creating a moral ambivalence, putting pressure on landlords and thereby creating conditions more favorable to the landless.

---

5. Shah, Kanti. "Vinoba's Bhoodan Movement: An Overview." https://www.mkgandhi.org/vinoba/anasakti/kantishah.htm, 2011.

6. McFadden, R. D. "Vinoba Bhave, A Gandhi Disciple and Social Reformer, Dies at 87." *New York Times*, November 16, 1982.

7. https://en.wikipedia.org/wiki/Bhoodan_movement

Dick served as a facilitator and fatherly inspiration for the Sarvodaya workers and for the villagers. Dick also established contacts with some donor agencies overseas. One agency in Germany whose concern was especially for children, sent money to build and staff *Balwadis*, child-care centers. These were established in *Gramdan* villages and other nearby villages. Dick also made contacts with one or two other donor agencies who sent money for agricultural implements and other farming needs in these villages.

On June 12, 1958 our second son Skyler was born in a hospital in Kodai. In October of that year, Jane, Hendrik, Skyler, and I were assigned to new work in the northwest corner of Madurai District in the village of Kallimandaiyam in Palani Taluk (township). At about the same time, Dick established a small Sarvodaya ashram a couple of miles west of Vatalagundu. It consisted of two thatched buildings, neatly kept, constructed like ordinary village buildings. As he was no longer Correspondent for the Vatalagundu Basic Training School, he made this ashram his headquarters. One reason for having located the ashram there was that there were several *Gramdans* nearby. So this way he could be close to the villagers who needed help while going through the big changes in their village life.

During this time I paid a visit to Dick at his Sarvodaya Ashram. One evening while I was there, there was a meeting with the local villagers; both Dick and one of his most trusted friends in the movement, S. Jaganathan, attended. Jaganathan was a young man of the Chettiyar (merchant) caste. A Hindu and a follower of Gandhi, he had dedicated his life to fighting non-violently for the poor farmers and the landless laborers. At the time of my visit, Jaganathan was the head of the Sarvodaya movement for all of Tamll Nadu (Madras State). A very unassuming and compassionate man of the Chettiyar caste, he had married a fine woman, Krishnammal, who was a Dalit.

One of the points of discussion during the evening meeting was the harvest of the peanuts in the field owned in common by the villagers. They decided that certain of the villagers would come and help to harvest the peanuts the following morning. The next morning, just a little after dawn, as I was getting ready to go home, I looked over at the field of peanuts that was ready for harvest, just across the road from the ashram. I could only see one figure there. As I came out of the building to get on my motorcycle I could see that the lone person who was harvesting the peanuts with his *manvatti* (short hoe) was none other than Jaganathan. I said "Hi" to him and went on my way on my motorcycle, inspired by the sight of this educated and genteel man who was going ahead with the harvest even though none of the villagers had shown up yet.

S. Jaganathan harvesting peanuts

At that time it was relatively rare for an educated Indian to do manual labor, for it was generally considered to be "beneath" people of that level. But that is the kind of leadership that Jaganathan demonstrated. And he was the type of person Dick associated with over and over again. Jaganathan, for his part, like many other young people who had been touched by Dick, was continually inspired by Keithahn's dedication, his example of simplicity and his identification with the poor.

When Dick went on leave to the USA in 1958 he left his jeep for me to use in my work in the Kallimandaiyam area. Although it was an old jeep, it was great having a four-wheeled vehicle, as we as a family had been making do with bicycles and public transportation (buses). I put the jeep to good use carrying bags of U.S. surplus (PL 480) grain (rice, wheat and corn) to the villages, which was needed because of a drought and the resulting poor crops early the following year. I also used the jeep to take government officials from the Palani Taluk (Township) around to villages so they could more quickly approve the digging of drinking-water wells for communities who either had no well, or whose wells had gone dry with the drought.

The floor of the Jeep was badly corroded and one could see the road through parts of it! So I decided that I would surprise Dick and have a new floor put in before he returned, which I did. But it took several trips to Dindigul and lots of patience with the body-repair shop there.

After he came back from furlough in the USA, Dick paid us several visits during the two years from 1959 to 1961, when we were living in Kallimandaiyam. It was always great to see him. I knew he'd always have some heartening word for us and some little joke; and he would always have interesting and inspiring stories about villagers he was working with, about his fellow Sarvodaya workers, or about church officers in the CSI with whom he was working. He had a fatherly and brotherly interest in each person he told us about, and would try to inspire each person to see a wider vision of working in some selfless way for India and India's poor.

A couple of times I went with Dick to the district headquarters, Madurai. We stayed with Sam and Suganthi Vairanapillai, an Indian Christian family and good friends of the Keithahns. They with their children had a modest house in the Sokkikulam part of Madurai. As there were no guest rooms in their home, Dick and I would just spread our bed sheets on their living-room floor, and have a very restful sleep, mosquitoes permitting! Sam had a PhD in Economics, I believe, and Suganthi had a Master's degree in Home Science. I believe that Suganthi got her degree from Columbia University and Sam got his last degree in the States also.

After finishing their education, the Vairanapillais wanted to come back to India and serve their people through the church. But things didn't work out that way, and Sam and Suganthi both felt that they had been frozen out of responsible positions in the church. Suganthi was a Christian Dalit, while Sam was from the "higher" caste of *Velalar,* not that that is supposed to matter once one becomes a Christian, but it seemed to. Being prevented from assuming responsible positions in the church made both of them a little bitter. Because of this, Dick would make a point of visiting them when he was in town to provide support and fellowship. They were very intelligent people, faithful to their Lord, and devoted to the Gandhian approach to the new society.

Beginning in the 1950s, Dick started to think about becoming an Indian citizen. I'm sure he felt that that would complete his identification with the cause of India. And by relinquishing his U.S. citizenship he would give up any special claim to privilege, the privilege that certainly does 'go with the territory' of being a foreign missionary. I'm not clear just when Dick changed his citizenship, but I think it was sometime during the period 1961–67.

Our family left India in April 1961, and when we returned to India in July 1967 to work with Action for Food Production (AFPRO), Dick was still at work in the Sarvodaya movement and still made his home base the Sarvodaya Ashram near Vatalagundu. My family and I were first stationed in New Delhi under AFPRO and after ten months we were transferred to Chennai city (Madras). As part of my job, I travelled to various places in India to investigate and evaluate the technical feasibility of proposed water-related development projects that might be funded by overseas donor agencies.

On one occasion in 1968, at Dick's request I visited a couple of villages near Vatalagundu where some land had been given to the landless or to the village to be held in common as a *Gramdan*. I remember one field of perhaps 20 or 30 acres that had two drawbacks: (1) the surficial soil was very sandy and stony, containing large gravel-sized stones; and (2) the land sloped significantly, perhaps 5 to 7 percent. Moreover, there was no hint of organic matter, and because of its coarse sandy, gravelly texture, the soil would not hold moisture long after a rain. I was pessimistic about using the land even for growing fruit trees, which Dick wanted to do. The only practical way to irrigate it would have been with sprinkler irrigation. I couldn't see the villagers' being able to afford a sprinkler irrigation system nor being sophisticated enough to operate the system wisely.

But Dick was adamant; he felt sure that some reasonable agricultural plan could be developed for the field. I think I may have said that the best thing to do would be to put it into native grasses and leave it for grazing for the village cows or goats, or some such thing. Dick had higher hopes for the land, and was a little annoyed and frustrated that I couldn't make more hopeful recommendations. But that's the way Dick was; he felt there was nothing which villagers working together couldn't accomplish. He was an unshakeable optimist.

I saw Dick only a few times during the four years I worked with AFPRO (1967–71). I had the feeling when we did meet that he considered me too much the over-schooled technician, caught up in theory and in the bureaucracy of a development agency, perhaps living and traveling too grandly, and, most importantly, too distant from ordinary poor people and from the realities of village life. On some points I had to agree. On others I felt that careful attention to the principles of irrigation, soil management, and water-well theory, were absolutely necessary for a successful agricultural enterprise, whether by a rich farmer or by a *Gramdan* village. Certainly AFPRO did not promote Gandhian principles as such; but we intended to be pragmatic. Still, very possibly we underrated what small farmers could do when they work together. At times I wondered whether Dick wasn't a little envious of my PhD degree, newly obtained in 1967. Sometimes he would mention that he had had an opportunity to go for his doctorate, but he had decided not to.

My family and I returned to the States in 1971. After we settled in New Jersey in 1972, I resumed my contact with Dick through correspondence. And a few times when Dick came home to visit his children and grandchildren, he stopped off in New Jersey and spent a few days with us. It was great. Of course it was wonderful to have news of India, particularly from his perspective. But also it was good to savor the old Keithahn energy, intensity, and commitment, moderated as they always were by his light touch of humor and humility. Sometimes we would have friends in to meet him, and most people really appreciated meeting him and hearing his stories of brave struggles in India.

On one occasion, I arranged for him to speak at my own Friends Meeting in Plainfield, New Jersey. Friends were interested to hear about his experiences, but even my best and most *simpatico* friends in the Meeting did not take to Dick as I did. Perhaps India was too far away and the problems and challenges of India too distant and difficult to visualize. I guess it is only for a few, those who hear *their* drummer, to recognize that rare soul who unceasingly marches to the same drummer. I did sometimes wonder, though, if Friends who pride themselves on following the Light within, weren't put off when they actually met someone who was living prophetically by the Light as Keithahn was, not merely just speaking truth to power, where many Quakers stop. Many of us Quakers like to stand by our principles, as long as we can have our comfortable life along with them.

During the mid- to late-1970s, Keithahn continued his Sarvodaya work at a reasonably high level, considering that he was about 80 years old. I remember his saying, "I think I am doing some of my best work these days," and he would be enthusiastic about one or another aspect of it. For example, there were the *Balwardis*, child-care centers, that he helped establish in

Bhoodan or *Gramdan* villages. There was also the work of reconciliation among villagers and castes, to which he also had a strong calling.

In January 1974, Dick wrote us how he had spent the recent Christmas season in Thanjavur in Tamil Nadu, helping the landless laborers obtain rights to cultivate lands belonging to the Hindu temples there. Thanjavur is a fairly conservative area, and the powers that be were opposed to leasing the temple land to the landless (usually Dalits). Dick wrote that men from the Communist party had first organized the landless people there, but that there was some violence in the course of an action in one village, and one of the landlord's men had been killed. In retaliation, early one morning 44 of the "outcaste" people were burned to death in a thatched cottage. No one went to prison for this dreadful crime, but six people were sentenced to prison for the killing of the landlord's man.

I quote from Dick's January 1974 letter to us:

> Jayaprakash Narayan, the great freedom and Gramdan leader of India, spent the Christmas week with us. He met many groups and people. We visited one of the main landlords of the area who has deep respect for Jayaprakash. This landlord promised to negotiate and get all of the cases out of the courts. Therefore, at 5:30 on Christmas morning the Sarvodaya workers very graciously joined me in an early Christmas morning prayer service. I do not know whether there was any Christian church service more devout than that. Then on our trip to meet the landlord involved in the promised arbitration, again we stopped in a little Cheri [outcaste section of a village] prayer chapel (Roman Catholic) to have a brief time in silence and in prayer. It had come to me recently that I could best pay my reverence to the Babe born in the manger in a Cheri and not in a 'palace church.' We also had a little to eat and then went on to the landlord.
>
> We all know that it will not be easy to negotiate with this man. In fact, he was almost non-cooperative during the first hour of our visit. However, slowly we touched his heart and a program for arbitration was set. Those of us involved planned to be in that area, January 3rd-13th hoping that we can reach a settlement before the meaningful Pongal holidays on January 14th. We seek your prayers.

Thus, the ministry of reconciliation proceeds at one little point in India. May this spirit and this movement of reconciliation go with us all throughout this New Year.

Dick came to see us in New Jersey for three days in the middle of September 1976. He was on his way back to India, having spent the late spring and summer with his son and daughter-in-law in Minnesota, where he also enjoyed a sizeable Keithahn reunion. He wrote in a card sent to us on June 15, 1976, a few weeks after he had arrived in Minnesota from India:

> And how are you all? Overfed, as I am getting overfed! Flew out of India 20th May; that same night, 11:30, Richard met me at Minneapolis Airport and we slept in an expensive hotel! How you spend the dollars!—much more than I do the rupees!—And still think you are poor. Returning to India about September 18th, am I going to see you? Near Washington, D.C.-> N.Y. railroad or N.Y.? And what are you doing? I think I am doing my best work yet—Frontier Balvadi and Health work. And I am pondering on the Universal-Eternal Christ. We put that Mystery too much in 'Jesus' and 'UCC' compounds! What do you think?! Blessings, Richard Benedict.

When Dick was with us for the few days in September 1976, we talked briefly about the possibility of our returning to India to work with the Sarvodaya Mandal in village water supply in Tamil Nadu. Then Dick wrote us on November 1, 1976, more specifically about that possibility:

> I have talked with [Sarvodaya] Mandal friends since my return and they are quite enthusiastic about such a possibility. There are many things that might be done. I am not sure how to proceed. I am very conscious of this whole situation; just now we are suffering a great deal in this and other areas because of a lack of rains and water in the wells. Even yesterday some 30 of us were talking about this general situation. Please indicate your own happy acceptance of such a proposal, and please indicate how we might proceed. I think that the [United Church Board for] World Ministries might well send you out just as they are sending the Riggses out to Oddanchatram. . . Do think about this, pray about it and let me know your reactions. Again, many, many thanks for all you did for me while I was there. How wonderful it was to be in your home again and with the children. May rich blessings be with each one of you.
> Sincerely, Dick

That opportunity brought forth an emotional exploration of whether or not we could happily return to India, especially if it meant my doing village-oriented work. In the end, I (we) had to say in essence that we weren't sure, but what it really meant, in essence, was 'no.' I have the feeling that

Dick knew that my letter, although not giving a categorical 'no,' meant we would not be taking him up his offer. And from that time until he came to pay us another visit in May 1980, we exchanged few letters. After I wrote to him in January 1977 and didn't hear back from him for some time, I had the feeling that he was quite disappointed. I gathered that he felt we had, in a sense, failed him, for perhaps he had hoped that I could to some extent begin to fill his shoes, to take from him the torch, before he left without having passed it on to any other Westerner, although, God knows, he had passed his torch to an untold number of wonderful Indian men and women.

In the late 1970s, Dick associated himself more and more with the Benedictine Order, whose brothers were working in the Vatalagundu-Periyakulam area. I believe he did take some kind of Benedictine vow, so he would sign himself as 'Richard Benedict,' his new Benedictine name.

The last two visits Dick paid us were in 1980. He was with us from May 3 to 10 and from October 20 to 24. These visits were at the beginning and at the end of one of his longest visits to the States. I picked Dick up at Kennedy Airport on May 3rd when he was just arriving from India. And I dropped him off at the Newark Airport on the 10th, whence he flew to the Midwest to see his children and grandchildren. I don't remember very much about that visit. It was probably pretty hectic here at home as we had seven Cambodian refugees living with us at the time, but I remember he seemed to enjoy them.

It was a pleasure to have Dick stay with us again on his way back to India. I remember meeting him at a bus stop on October 20. On the 24th, we drove him to Kennedy Airport to see him off. That was his last visit to the States before he died. I knew then that I would be leaving within a few weeks to go to Egypt for more than a year to participate in a development study project in Sinai for my company, Dames & Moore. Dick seemed enthusiastic about that prospect and also encouraged me in the limited ministry I felt I could undertake here in America.

For the next 18 months, I was fully occupied with and engrossed in the water-resources assessment of Sinai in Egypt. I worked mostly in Cairo with short trips to the Sinai. I must have written Dick at least one or two letters between November 1980 and April 1982, when the Sinai Development report was complete.

Sometime between 1980 and 1983, the Thariens of the Oddanchatram Christian Fellowship Hospital set up a house for Dick where he could make his headquarters and, at the same time, be under the tender and competent care of Dr. Tharien and other doctors there at the Hospital. So, Dick moved his headquarters from the Sarvodaya Ashram near Vatalagundu to the Fellowship at Oddanchatram.

They built for him a small one-room building only about 150 feet from the Thariens' home. Until close to the end, he would walk to the Thariens' house to take his meals with them. During this period, Dick had the use of an old sedan car; he had given up his jeep earlier. Sam, a young Indian Christian, was his driver, as well as his typist and social secretary. Sam and his wife would commonly stay with Dick through the night. Sam and the Thariens always referred to Dick as 'Keithahnji,' a term of endearment and respect, as did many other of Dick's Indian colleagues and friends.

In the fall of 1983, I found out through a mutual friend, Charlie Ryerson, who had been an Oberlin College representative in Madurai in the 1950s, that Dick was ill. In late January 1984, I put a call through to Oddanchatram and talked to Mrs. Tharien. We had a bad connection, but I was able to grasp that at age 85, Dick was relatively weak, though not seriously ill, and that he was mentally alert.

I pondered this news and finally decided that it was the right time to go to see him before it was too late. So within two weeks, I arranged for vacation from my company, enticed Jeremy, my Oddanchatram 'baby', to come with me (he was between jobs), and arranged for the visas and airline tickets. Everything went smoothly, and by the middle of February we were in India! We landed in Bombay, got to Oddanchatram by plane, train and bus, and we walked from the bus stand to the Christian Fellowship Hospital, which had changed significantly since 1971. There were many more staff people and buildings than there had been 13 years before and there were luxuriant trees everywhere. It looked like a little Kerala!

Whom should we see first inside the compound on his cycle wearing a white jibba and dhoti but Dr. Tharien! He was surprised and pleased to see us, as he had not yet received my letter announcing our visit. When we told him that we had come to see Keithahnji, he informed us that Dick had left for Madras by train the previous day or two to attend a meeting and would be away for three days.

Jeremy and I decided to go up to Kodaikanal and spend two of the three days there. But we made sure we came back to the Fellowship in Oddanchatram the evening before Dick was to arrive. I was in contact with Dick's secretary, Sam, who was to meet Dick in the early morning. He agreed to take us with him to Dindigul to meet the train.

Sam woke us up at about 4 AM, and we quickly got ready and piled into the little car. At the Dindigul station, the wait seemed endless. The train from Madras was late, but it did come in the end, and we found the third-class car where Dick was. As he was getting out of the carriage, I offered him a hand (he was using a cane). When he saw who was greeting him, he said with a smile, "Well, what are *you* doing here?" I knew he was happy to see Jeremy and me. I said, "We came to see *you*, Dick," to which he replied with a grin something like, "It seems like nonsense to me."

Instead of driving from the train station to Oddanchatram, as would have seemed sensible given the long third-class train ride and Dick's age, we went straight to nearby Gandhigram. While Dick was speaking with colleagues there about matters of his work, I visited a couple of classes in the master's program in peace studies, which included a discussion of Gandhiji's efforts to bring peace between Muslims and Hindus in Bengal after independence.

We ate supper that evening with the Thariens, and what a treat that was. All the meal times at the Thariens, those three days with Dick and Tharien were memorable. There were a lot of reminiscences, and each story Dick told was exciting and, at the same time, hopeful—hopeful for the downtrodden and for India. It was great to hear stories of his past meetings with Gandhiji and other Congress leaders. At one mealtime, I remember I asked him whether he had seen the movie "Gandhi." I was surprised when he said he had seen it, and when he said:

Dr. Tharien and Dick at supper when Jeremy and I visited them in February 1984

"You know, I never fully realized to what extent Gandhiji suffered until I saw that movie." This was Keithahn, who had probably known Gandhi as intimately as any Westerner had, with the possible exception of Rev. C. F. Andrews!

One night at supper, I remember Dick's telling us about a recent struggle in a village where the women doing agricultural work were asking for equal pay for equal work, or close to it. And there were no men to take up their cause. Keithahnji urged his fellow Sarvodaya workers and the male villagers to take seriously the women's cause (demand). I can't remember the details of this case, which was more complicated than I've stated it. But it was 'vintage Dick' for him to see instantly to the heart of a moral Issue, while others would still be scratching their heads trying to figure out what the ethical issue was, and if there was one, whether it was worth rocking the boat over!

One evening, Dick accompanied Jeremy and me in his car to Navakani, a village near Kallimandaiyam, in which I had done some work. (In 1960, I had taken the government contract to dig a public drinking-water well for the Dalit Christians of the village). The Christians wanted to have a "little" reception for us. The local CSI pastor, Rev. Anburaj, and his wife came along too. It was great fun, especially to see the faces of the people whom I had earlier tried to help. Their lives had improved in the 23 years since we left that village area, mostly because of their own efforts. I had always observed that the young Dalit men of that village had that certain oomph and light in their eyes, so I was not surprised to see how far they had advanced themselves. Some of them had jobs in the government electric power department.

The time in Oddanchatram with Dick, the Thariens, and other friends at the Fellowship went by too quickly. But Jeremy and I wanted to visit a few other friends in Kerala, Madurai, and Chennai before returning to the States. Dick's mind was very clear. However, his physical weakness was evident in the use of his cane, the slowness and deliberateness of his walk, and in the rather long afternoon naps he would take.

I wrote to Dick on March 6th, soon after Jeremy and I returned home. And Dick answered on March 20; it was my last letter from him. His response started with a prayer or poem, "Blessed is the Home." He thanked Jeremy and me for coming to spend time with him, although he didn't want to admit that we had explicitly come out to see *him*! The understatement of the century was his saying in the letter, "Yes, I do wish that you and some of the family might come again to India. I always find it a very interesting place to be." An *interesting* place to be? It was the very lifeblood of his soul! India was the only source of stimulation and challenge that really mattered to him.

I had no word from India after that until mid-December 1984. A Christmas greeting from our friend, J. E. Sokkiah, a retired mission worker in Madurai, mentioned that Dick had died peacefully at Oddanchatram that month. Later, we learned that Dick died on December 7th after a short period when his health had steadily declined despite all the medical care and supportive measures. His body was buried on the Christian Hospital Fellowship property in Oddanchatram, marked with a simple engraved tombstone.

A SHORT CHRONOLOGY OF HIS LIFE[8]

Ralph Richard Keithahn was born in Martin County, Minnesota, on January 29, 1898. As he was growing up, he helped his father on the family's 320-acre farm. To help with the farm work most years they had a hired man, as Dick recounts in his memoir.[9] One of these was Tony Zobroski, a Polish Roman Catholic who lacked some of the standards of the Keithahns' German-American culture. He was illiterate and Dick helped to teach him to read and write. Tony was fully accepted by the family. He slept with Dick, and Dick's mother washed and mended his clothes. Dick considered him one of his best friends. As Dick notes in his memoir, the training he received through Tony and the way his parents treated Tony were "perhaps more important than any I received in educational institutions. And, friendship with such people has cleared the way for friendship with our simple, needy, illiterate villagers in India."

Dick recounts in his memoir that when he was 13 and had just completed his confirmation in the German Lutheran church in which he was raised, the pastor told him, "You have done well. God has given you special talents. I do not know how you can use them better than being a missionary to India." Dick notes that "Thus, in my fourteenth year, my vocation was decided."[10] He would meet many other Christian leaders later in his formative years who would inspire him and lead him into his prophetic calling. In his memoir,[11] he describes those who had been particularly important in furthering his resolve to witness in India the way he did; to name just a few: professors at Carleton college, the Chicago Theological Seminary and Yale University; missionaries to China and Africa; speakers at meetings of

---

8. Much of the information in this section was provided to me by Dick's older daughter Dr. Mearl Marie Keithahn.

9. Keithahn, *Pilgrimage in India*, 7.

10. Keithahn, *Pilgrimage in India*, 3.

11. Keithahn, *Pilgrimage in India*, 5–10.

the Student Volunteer Movement, including Dr. Walter Judd and Sherwood Eddy; and, inspiring Indian Christian leaders.

Dick worked his way through Carleton College in Northfield, Minnesota, mostly through physical work. After graduating from Carleton in 1920, he attended the Chicago Theological Seminary (CTS) and earned a Bachelor of Divinity. While in Chicago, he became the president of the Student Volunteer Movement for missionary work. The vice-president was a medical student named Mildred McKie. In working together, they discovered their common interest and outlook and would later share their life together. Dick was ordained as a clergyman in 1922. He went on to Yale University, where he obtained an MA in Education in 1925.

Dick first came to India in 1925 as a young missionary under the American Board of Commissioners for Foreign Missions (ABCFM).[12] He thus became the newest member of the American Madura Mission (AMM)[13], which then numbered 80 men and women.[14] After completing his Tamil language study, Dick became the Correspondent (Manager) of the AMM Teacher Training School in Pasumalai, a suburb of Madurai in Madras State. In 1929, Dick paid a visit to Gandhi's Sabarmathi Ashram in Ahmedabad Gujarat, to have a closer look at the Mahatma and spend some time with him. This was the ashram Gandhi started in 1917 (also known as 'Harijan[15] Ashram'), which he made his headquarters from 1917 to 1930. Dick soon began to identify himself with the Independence movement and invited followers of Gandhi and the Congress party into his bungalow quarters in Pasumalai. The British rulers and most of the other missionaries looked askance at that. I believe he was warned several times about this by fellow missionaries, including John X. Miller, who was a leader of the mission work in Pasumalai in those days. But to Keithahn, Gandhi had become the embodiment of India's political, social, and religious ideals. Following Gandhi's lead, he began to wear home-spun *khadi* clothes because 'it was made by the needy poor people in the villages.'

---

12. The ABCFM was the missionary board for the Congregational churches. In India they had established the American Madura Mission in Madurai District of Tamil Nadu, and the American Marathi Mission centered in the Ahmednagar area of Maharashtra, western India.

13. Since Independence in 1947, the city and district is known as 'Madurai', its Tamil name, rather than Madura.

14. Compared to just ten of us in 1970, four of whom were stationed in Madras and were unassociated with the work of the Madurai-Ramnad Diocese!

15. Harijan, meaning 'People of God', was the name Gandhi applied to people belonging to outcaste groups. Now the preferred word for Harijan across the board is 'Dalit'.

EPILOGUE

The home-spinning of cotton and then weaving it into fabric in small village-level 'mills,' as advocated by Gandhi, was also a tactic used to assist the independence movement. For it deprived the cotton mills in Manchester and Lancashire, England of many of its Indian customers. Until then, Britain would export raw cotton grown in India to England, where it would be processed in their large cotton mills. Indians were used to buying the resulting English-produced fabric for their own clothing, thus depriving themselves of the income which should have accrued to them had they used local, village-level, hand-operated spinning and weaving machines.

In 1930, the Madurai Collector (the British administrator of Madurai District) named J. F. Hall became aware of Keithahn's support for the pro-independence Congress Party, particularly after Dick had organized a meeting attended by both Pasumalai teachers and members of the Congress Party. And then when Hall learned that Congress Party members had garlanded Keithahn at the Madurai train station, Hall decided to take action. He asked for Keithahn to come see him; he reminded Dick that he (Dick) had signed a 'pledge of neutrality' as a condition of his being permitted to work in India as a non-British missionary. The pledge said that he would not engage in political activity in India.

Hall then threatened the American Madura Mission that if they did not take action against Keithahn by sending him out of India, the AMM's requests for government's grants for its schools would be ignored. AMM Secretary John Banninga met with Collector Hall, who pointed to the pile of documents sitting on his desk. "These are requests for grants from your mission, and they will not leave my desk until Keithahn is out of the country," he said. The AMM Interim Committee decided to favor the ongoing work of their various educational institutions over a political commitment to the nationalist movement. They voted to send Keithahn out of the country. But Keithahn and a couple of others in the Mission fervently believed that the poor village people could improve their lot only after the country achieved its independence.

Because of the AMM vote, Keithahn left India on July 26, 1930. Back in America, he got in touch with Mildred McKie, whom he had worked with and admired when they were students from 1920 to 1922. In 1930 Mildred was finishing up her medical training. She and Dick married in Chicago in 1931. Mildred had to complete her internship as an MD in New York, so Dick did Missionary Fellowship studies at Union Theological Seminary during that time. The next year the couple started serving as Home Missionaries in South Dakota, and during this period Mearl Marie and Richard were born. But Dick and Mildred had been planning to go to the foreign mission field ever since their days at CTS. And in 1935, the family moved to India under the ABCFM.

But the ABCFM and AMM were unwilling to accept Mildred and Dick as *full* missionaries, but only as Associate Missionaries, working without a salary. The Keithahns chose Devakottai in Ramnad as their field of service, where Dick worked on a welfare program for the Dalits, and Mildred was in charge of a health-care program. But in 1937, Dick and Mildred severed ties with the American Madura Mission because of their belief that Indian leaders should be taking over the leadership of the mission organization faster and because Dick questioned the over-institutionalization of the work.

That year they moved to Bangalore, where the family lived in a Gandhian-style ashram, the Ananda Ashram on Bannerghatta Road, and Dick started working in the slums and trained college students to do the same. He also organized the Social Workers Brotherhood and was instrumental in forming the Youth Christian Council of Action, which stimulated the youth of the churches to rise up against injustice and corruption in the society.

In Bangalore, the Keithahn family lived simply, not far above the poverty level. This was to show their friendship and oneness with their Indian colleagues. They were supported only by informal donations from friends, family, and a few churches back home. Ruth Seabury of the ABCFM visited the Keithahns there, I believe, in the late 1930s. She was concerned that they were living so simply that the family appeared to be having difficulty making ends meet. So Ruth petitioned the Board to provide a subsistence allowance for the Keithahns. The Board agreed and the Keithahns accepted, thereby becoming something like associate missionaries of the Board. In 1939 while they were in Bangalore, their third child, Ruth Kirubai, was born.

After a few years in Bangalore, Dick again began to associate himself openly with the Independence movement of the Congress Party. Many times this work took him away from Bangalore. He became a close friend and follower of Mohandas (Mahatma) Gandhi, and he became convinced of the power of non-violence in his own life as a Christian. In 1944 the government of India (British) and the government of Mysore (the province where Bangalore was) asked him and his family to leave India again, saying that they were "disturbing the peace of India." The British police escorted the family out of India. In Bombay, before boarding their ship to the U.S., they went to meet Gandhi, who gave them his blessings and remarked, "Keithahn, you are a smart fellow. When you wanted a free passage to your home country, you cleverly managed to have the British Government pay for it. I am sure you will return to a free India soon!"

144 EPILOGUE

During the subsequent interim period in the U.S., Dick was posted to work at the Merom Institute in Merom, Indiana, a small town on the Wabash River. There he was assigned by the mission board to work in an ongoing program to strengthen the rural church in the Bible belt of southern Indiana and Illinois.

In 1947, when India achieved independence, C. Rajagopalachari, the first Governor-General of independent India, cabled the Keithahns, "Welcome to a free India." This time the ABCFM was willing to recognize the Keithahns as associate missionaries, and soon they were on their way back to India.

Although Dick and Mildred were now members of the American Madura Mission, a few of their fellow missionaries were doubtful of the orthodoxy of Dick's faith. After all, he sometimes participated (experimented) in inter-faith worship, in which Hindus, Muslims, and at least one Christian were present! This and his willingness to do without many everyday comforts made many of his colleagues in the mission feel uneasy. But his fellow ABCFM missionaries, the Heinemans in Pasumalai and the Riggses in Ramnad district, probably didn't feel uncomfortable about Dick and Mildred's voluntary poverty at all, as they were busily setting their own standards for simple living. I think that most of the missionaries in the Madura Mission did not want to judge Dick harshly.

One of Dick's dreams was to start a Gandhian Training Institute in South India. In 1947 he and Mildred started to assist T. S. Soundram of the TVS family and her husband G. Ramachandran in establishing Gandhigram. It was a rural development center located near Dindigul in Madurai District. Gandhigram was founded on the principle of "basic education," the educational philosophy of Gandhiji[16] that emphasized educating village children so that they would be encouraged to stay in the villages where they grew up by providing the tools to help them thrive. The tools would involve using productive and straightforward technologies, including spinning cotton yarn and weaving to create cotton fabrics.

In Gandhigram, Dick devoted his time to the training program and the improvement of the center. Dick's Christian witness in Gandhigram was such that many people believed he was instrumental in the conversion of several people to Christianity. But the diocesan authorities believed that his close association with other religions in Gandhigram could cause misunderstandings, so they temporarily withheld Dick's privilege of performing the sacraments. In this complex situation, Dick ultimately decided it was best for him to withdraw from Gandhigram, which he did in 1956.

16. *Gandhiji* is the term of endearment for Gandhi.

Meanwhile, Mildred continued her care of Mearl Marie, Richard, and Ruth, while practicing medicine in rural clinics. She also began to research indigenous medicine in rural India, about which she would later write a book.

At this time, the Christian Fellowship Hospital was taking shape in Oddanchatram on the western side of Madurai District. It was made up of young Christian medical professionals from the neighboring state of Kerala. These young professionals had formed a mission fellowship group when they were in medical school and had dedicated themselves to perform medical service in a needy area in Tamil Nadu. The group was led by Dr. A. K. Tharien[17]. The medical center and small hospital started in 1955 in a dilapidated house with a few thatched sheds. It grew to become a substantial hospital in Oddanchatram with a smaller adjunct hospital at Ambilikai, four miles north, for leprosy, tuberculosis, and cancer patients. The Fellowship also had outreach health and development programs covering about thirty villages in and around Oddanchatram.

Dick was in contact with the group and was instrumental in their choosing Oddanchatram to set up a rural hospital. As he said in his memoir,[18] "I suggested Oddanchatram but told them to consult Bishop Lesslie Newbigin, then Bishop of Madurai-Ramnad Diocese. Bishop Newbigin suggested that Ramnad District was the more needy area. I agreed but said to my young friends, 'You want to be self-sufficient. I think there is a possibility of this in the Palani-Dindigul area with your center in Oddanchatram; Ramnad District is so poor and backward that you will not be able to be self-reliant.' I had my doubts even about the Oddanchatram area. I had not realized that this group could have such an influence upon people—that they would be able to support a first-rate hospital as well as they have."

In the 1950s, the marriage of Dick and Mildred sadly started to weaken. There was a series of reconciliations and separations until 1959 when the separation was final, and Mildred moved back to the U.S., where among other things she held classes and seminars in nutrition and naturopathy.

In the late fifties, India caught the world's attention because of the Sarvodaya Movement inspired by Gandhi. Vinoba Bhave (Vinobaji) requested that Dick be the Chairman of the All India Bhoodan Conference as he was above sectarian interest. For the next ten years, Dick concentrated his

---

17. Please see the chapter devoted to Tharien in the main part of this book.
18. Keithahn, *Pilgrimage in India*, 36.

attention on this program of *Bhoodan* and *Gramdan*[19] as the socio-economic foundation of a real Sarvodaya society.

Bhoodan Acts were subsequently passed in several states that stated that the beneficiary, or beneficiaries, had no right to sell the land or use it for non-agricultural purposes or forestry. For example, Section 25 of the Maharashtra State Bhoodan Act states that the beneficiary, who must be landless, should use the land only for subsistence cultivation.

During this period, poor farmers and landless laborers were awakened in some locations against injustice and exploitation. In one case, Dick took the lead to get the release of unlawfully-held temple land in the village of Vilampatti. The police arrested him and put him in the Madurai Prison for a week. During that week, the Government finally released the land for those poor farmers and landless laborers to cultivate.

When Dick reached his mid-seventies, he decided to retire from active service and allow younger Indian colleagues to take over. He wanted to spend most of his time in deeper spiritual contemplation. During this period, the Nashdom Abbey near London, England, confirmed him as an Anglican Benedictine Oblate.

Dick received an honorary doctorate on June 12, 1970, at Carleton College's commencement. Upon presenting him with the degree, the President of the college remarked, among other things, that

> As a Christian missionary, you have gained respect from Muslim and Hindu alike. American by origin, you are now Indian in spirit. In an affluent world you have chosen the life of simplicity. From the farms of southern Minnesota, you have shared your knowledge, experience and strength with the farmers of India. Your College is proud of you; we stand taller because of your magnanimity of spirit.

M. M. Thomas from Kerala, India, was one of Keithahn's students in Bangalore during 1941–42. He later became a well-regarded ecumenical theologian and articulator of Indian Christian nationalism. In his foreword to Dick's Book: *Pilgrimage in India: An Autobiographical Fragment*[20], Thomas wrote on how the poor shaped Keithahn's priorities and the way in which Keithahn challenged the Christian community:

---

19. A *Gramdan* is a village where almost all the farmers of the village donated land to the landless because of Vinoba Bhave, and then those donated lands were cultivated together by the previously landless villagers.

20. Keithahn, *Pilgrimage in India*, viii.

> Guru Keithahn's sole concern was that we should be committed to the cause of the under-privileged, especially of the villages of India...Brother Dick has been critical of the Christian Institute for the Study of Religion and Society (CISRS) [which M. M. Thomas led]—and legitimately so. He feels that we have not been sufficiently concerned with the study of village situations and that we have not promoted Christian action in the villages. This, of course, is part of his disappointment with—and challenge to—the whole Indian church.

Dick died on December 7, 1984, in Oddanchatram after a short period when his health had steadily declined despite all the medical care and supportive measures. He was buried on the property of the Christian Hospital Fellowship in Oddanchatram.

Keithahn's birth centenary was celebrated on January 27, 1998, in Oddanchatram and Dindigul in Madurai District. *The Hindu*, a respected South Indian English newspaper, reported on the celebration:

> Rev. Ralph Richard Keithahn was a Christian missionary, who saw Christ in Mahatma Gandhi after coming to India. Attracted by the principles of "truth and non-violence," Keithahn transformed himself into a "Gandhian missionary" and served the country for over 50 years. According to Mr. S. Jaganathan, Sarvodaya leader, who hails Keithahn as his "spiritual father," the missionary's life is a saga of devoted service, especially to the downtrodden. He valued women's development, education of children, and communal amity as essential to the overall development of the society.

HIS VIEWS ON CONVERSION AND INTER-FAITH DIALOGUE

Dick opposed any kind of 'mass conversion,' or any conversion tainted by material considerations, as exemplified by the conversion of an entire caste group (usually Dalit) in a village. His position was often misinterpreted to mean that there was no justification for conversion of *any* type. Bishop Newbigin firmly took issue with his position on mass conversion, for he saw in it a danger to Christianity and a contradiction. For to him and many other churchmen and churchwomen, Christianity has as a central part of its *raison d'etre* the going forth, sharing our faith and bringing unbelievers to Christ. But for Keithahn, this more orthodox approach involved the greater danger of violating the sense of mutual respect among people, without which no human relationship, religious or otherwise, can flourish.

Writing probably in the 1950s, Dick and G. Ramachandran in "Conversion and Fellowship," said: "Every human being has the right to grow in one's own moral and spiritual tradition, and any attempt to uproot a human being out of such a background must be treated as unholy." The statement clearly came out against forced conversions and those induced by material gifts. It also opposed the insistence of evangelists that non-Christians must accept the traditional absolute claims of Christianity. But it did recognize the validity of sincere, unforced conversions: "there will always be truthful and earnest men and women who will cross the borderlines of their own moral and spiritual traditions seeking fulfillment through a change which grows within." But the real benefit of the meeting of equals through inter-religious dialogue, which Dick and Ramachandran would have us take note of, is the "glorious interchange of ideas, values, and truths among all the great moral and spiritual traditions of the world." This concept led Dick to participate in, or experiment with, inter-religious worship experiences.

HIS LEADERSHIP IN THE KODAIKANAL ASHRAM FELLOWSHIP

The Kodaikanal Ashram Fellowship was started in 1934 by a few missionaries who were inspired by Rev. E. Stanley Jones's ashram in North India. A few years later, Dick Keithahn assumed primary responsibility for the Kodai Ashram, and he continued in that role nearly until he died in 1984. Kodaikanal is in the mountains (the Western Ghats of India), and the city is some 7,000 feet in elevation, and so it was a very pleasant place to vacation and have retreats during the hot season (April and May).

The ashram fellowship was managed by a Board, which included Indian Christian laypeople and professionals, including J. Vedasiromani of Palamkottai in Tirunelveli District (just south of Madurai District) and Henry Periyanayagam of Madurai. As I saw it, the ashram fellowship served three functions:

- It was a place where Indians and foreigners, people often of very different economic means, could come together for a few days or several weeks to live, learn and worship in a close family-like environment;
- It was a place for the sharing of different religious traditions; and,
- It was a place to come for rest, quiet, and a deepening of spiritual life.

Wednesdays were the quiet days at the Kodaikanal Ashram, when there was no speaking of any kind, not even at meals. This was to foster inward stillness and meditation. Dick and other members of the Board prepared an exciting program for the remaining days of the week for the entire nine weeks that constituted 'the season' in April and May. Spiritual leaders in the Christian church and Hindu or Muslim spiritual leaders were invited to speak as a part of the program. It was most stimulating and pleasant to rub shoulders with Indians on an equal basis.

The ashram had a Christian perspective at its root, but non-Christians were welcome to participate fully and sometimes take part in periods of prayer and meditation. The strict vegetarian diet of the ashram also helped to encourage vegetarian Hindus to come and take part. Ashram life involved the sharing of housework tasks, including house cleaning and food preparation. The cost of staying at the ashram was graduated based on people's ability to pay.

Dick considered the ashram his home when in Kodai; he never accepted a mission bungalow in which to spend his "vacation." To stay in the mission bungalows in Kodai would have set him apart from his Indian friends, as most of them could never afford to stay in such surroundings. It also would have meant that he would have had to forego the satisfying reality of community he had helped to develop at the ashram. Dick would often make trips up to Kodai out of season to check on the ashram buildings and confer with his friend Ramasamy and his family, who were the caretakers of the ashram and its grounds.

In the mid-1950s, when we first knew her, Mildred lived almost year-round in a part of East House, one of the mission bungalows in Kodai. Their daughter Ruth was in high school at the Kodai School, so Mildred stayed there partly for her.

HIS MINISTRY OF RECONCILIATION

Dick took 'reconciliation' as one of the most important parts of his mission as a Christian. He worked with other friends trying to reconcile two of the factions in Kerala's Syrian Orthodox church. Part of the urgency for this was the lawsuit that had been brought forth, with both of the two factions laying claim to significant amounts of church property. Dick would help set up meetings with representatives of the two factions and sit down with them and other fair-minded Christian friends. To my knowledge, these efforts never stopped the progress of the lawsuit, but it certainly wasn't because Dick and his friends hadn't tried.

There was a Christian ashram at Thadagam established by Bishop Pakenham-Walsh in the foothills of the Western Ghats near Coimbatore in Tamil Nadu. I visited the ashram once and enjoyed the sense of peace and beauty there. I believe the reason the ashram had been established in the first place was to promote discussion between these two factions of the Syrian Orthodox church and to provide an atmosphere where mutual understanding could develop. Dick often visited that ashram to lend moral support and to see friends there.

Another example of Dick's drive toward reconciliation was his several days' visit to Ramnad District in 1957. He went with his associates to bring about reconciliation between two castes in conflict with each other. He visited villages there soon after a terrible outbreak of violence in September 1957 between the *Maravar* caste and the *Pallar* Dalit caste.

The *Pallar* Dalits had improved themselves in recent years by finding better-paying work and seeing that their children were better educated. And many of them in that area had converted to Christianity. The *Maravars*, on the other hand, comprised a robber caste, actually 'broad-day-light robbers,' but were also farmers making up the largest landowning caste in the district, as opposed to the so-called 'night-time' robbers, the *Kallars,* who mostly lived in Madurai District.

The Maravars were mostly Hindus, 'caste Hindus' at that, so they considered themselves a cut above the local Dalits. I don't remember what started the violence between the two groups, but there was a lot of it. There were cases of the Maravars firing rounds of shots into churches where they suspected or knew that the Dalits were worshiping. When we were visiting the Riggses in Ramnad District in 1957, I saw the bullet holes in two or three church buildings and charred church doors in one village.

During Dick's work with the *Bhoodan* or *Gramdan* movement led by Vinoba Bhave, reconciliatory action often had to be taken within villages where significant land holdings had been donated to the landless poor. Disagreements would arise over parcel boundaries, over loans, and the cultivation of the common lands. Dick and other *Bhoodan* workers would work to help the people reach agreements.

HIS MISSION TO HIS FRIENDS

Dick regularly wrote to his friends in India and across the world. He felt he had a mission to show them how far Christ's teachings could carry one if one were but obedient. He felt, I believe, he had a mission to serve as an example of what Christian discipleship could be and to inspire his friends to do the same, or more.

Many of his letters would begin with a free-verse poem that would represent a prayer or a plea. The following poem entitled "Spirituality and Integrity—From the Rock of Vision" was written in late 1976 and appeared in a letter he wrote to me on November 1, 1976. (The 'Rock of Vision' is a big flat rock, part of a cliff overlooking Periyakulam and the rest of the plains below, at which evening and morning vespers at the Kodai ashram were held.):

> Are we not coming to a new Integrity with the Hindu, Buddhist, Muslim and all—'unto the very last?'
> So we start our Gandhi Fortnight pilgrimage to our Gramdan villages in the Batlagundu [Vatalagundu] area on Jan. 29th.
> Such yatras [journeys] are going on in many parts of India:
> At Sarvodaya Ashram the training of exploited but dedicated villagers has started
> Taking this revolution to 'One Humanity' a step farther.
> Less than 10 percent use over half of the world's natural resources.
> A minority use most of the seafood resources. In their affluence they seriously pollute the world. Millions of us profess allegiance to those who say,
> 'Seek ye first the Kingdom of God and His Righteousness!'
> Does not this discipleship need to be reassessed?
> Must this not begin with all spiritual Ministry?
> 'Do justly, love mercy, walk humbly with Truth.'
> Does this not mean 'stripping: as Gandhi went to the loincloth?
> For the Kingdom's sake?
> Must we not go beyond professionalism everywhere?
> Must we not keep near to Mother Earth and its healing processes?
> Must we not come nearer to one another—to Koinonia?
> Must we not remember 'the earth Is the Lord's;' Give the land to the tiller; tools to the laborer?
> True, done non-violently, but with insistence!
> Is there not injustice at every door?
> As we walk through our villages, we often find cesspools, drains at every door.
> Is this not cleanliness compared with *our* filth?

Did not the Master Jesus leave the plains of loving service?
Go up to the cross on Calvary? and then 'rise again!'
Have we such faith, courage, and commitment?
Should not *all* of *us* be on trek?
'Going out not knowing where we go?'
And must we not go *together*?
A new spirituality, shepherding of the flock, sharing:
A new method, evangelism, mission, and adventurous living.
Many are on trek, and you?
Daringly, Ralph Richard Keithahn

HIS INFLUENCE ON YOUNG CHRISTIANS AND HINDUS

Dick had a considerable influence on young Indian Christians (and non-Christians) through the Student Christian Movement. Dr. Tharien likes to tell the story of how he (Tharien) and a few other Christian friends were close to, or actually in, the Communist movement in Kerala when they were students in college. They felt that only the Communists had the answer to the gross inequities they saw all around them, that their church seemed to have no interest in righting. Then they came to hear Keithahnji when he would speak at college gatherings, and they immediately sensed his sincerity and the fact that he lived what his words said. They also perceived that here was a missionary who was *with* them in every sense of the word.

What evolved out of this experience of meeting Keithahn and other Christians in the Independence Movement at the college where Tharien attended in Miraj, Maharashtra, was a unique Christian fellowship. These Christian students came together for prayer to seek God's guidance for their current and future lives. The question they sought answers to was how best they could serve God's people when they finished their medical education.

The Oddanchatram Christian Fellowship Hospital was one of the essential manifestations, or answered prayers, coming out of this Christian prayer group at that college. And the first doctors who started the Fellowship's hospital were Tharien (Dr. A. K. Tharien), Dr. Jacob Cherian, and his wife, Dr. Mary Cherian. As mentioned earlier, Dick guided the group in the selection of the location for the Fellowship to begin its service. So in 1955, the Fellowship started its excellent work at Oddanchatram, under the simplest of conditions. It was established in the hope that they would be given the necessary strength and love and be provided with the resources they needed to tend to the sick and suffering in that area.

Dick also had an enormous influence on many young (and older) Hindu and Muslim friends. His unwavering loyalty to the Independence Movement and his uncompromising respect for Gandhiji brought him many permanent friendships. Moreover, his Hindu and Muslim friends appreciated his insistence that people of all religious persuasions must be respected equally. One of Dick's most loyal Hindu friends was S. Jaganathan, about whom I wrote earlier in this chapter. Jaganathan and his colleagues looked up to Dick for advice and guidance and for that inspiration without which an 'impossible dream'-type movement like the *Gramdan* movement was almost bound to fail.

And he didn't fail them. I wonder whom they look up to now of comparable age and wisdom and dedication. I have no doubt there are Indians of that stature who are close to the Sarvodaya movement but having been out of India for so long, I don't know of them. The proof of the pudding is in the eating. Dick is not known by his Indian friends to have been a great Christian missionary, even though he was that. No, he is remembered affectionately, as being one of them, like a father. He is remembered as 'Keithahnji.'

THE SIMPLICITY OF DICK'S LIFE

One of the first things I remember about Dick was what he wrote to me at Hartford Theological Seminary while Jane and I were taking training in missions before we first came to India. Someone had given me his address, telling me that he was one missionary I should sit up and pay attention to. So I wrote to Dick and got an air letter back, but he made it clear in his reply that the poor with whom he was identifying could not afford airmail letters so that thereafter he would have to write to me via the cheaper sea-mail post.

Another thing that comes to mind took place several years later. I was traveling with Dick and other Indian friends near Tirunelveli. We had stopped for the night with friends. In the morning we took our baths as usual. When I reached for my towel in my bag, I found it was still wet or moist from the day before. When I mentioned this to Dick, he suggested that I give up having a towel at all and either make do with the day's dhoti or wait until I air-dried! Indeed, I never saw him carrying towels around on his trips!

Just how simply did Dick live? Pretty simply. How simple is simple? He had an automobile or jeep during the years I knew him (1956 and later).

Did his use of a car mean that he wasn't living simply? In a way, yes. But the assumption is that his work justified it and that he could accomplish much more for the poor with a vehicle than without one. All that is arguable. To me, though, his having a car did not interfere with his witness, nor mar his commitment to the poor, nor his dedication to bring justice forward for all.

In almost all other ways, Dick lived simply by anyone's definition. He always wore only khadi (hand-spun) cloth. He had it tailored so that, at least on the plains, he wore shorts and a simple short-sleeved collarless shirt. The colors could vary, but I seem to remember his wearing a blue combination most commonly. For formal gatherings, he frequently wore the familiar South Indian *dhoti* and *jibba*.

His meals were simple also. And he sometimes replaced his simple fare with a day, or several days, of fasting. He was a vegetarian. When he stayed with friends in private homes or institutions, he was usually treated to some of the best of South Indian vegetarian cooking. When he cooked for himself, he would often boil up some whole grains, such as *cholam, ragi, thenai*, or *kumbu*, all very nutritious native millets, but of varying degrees of attractiveness to western and urban-Indian palates. With the whole grains, he would have raw, fresh vegetables and fruit. And that would be all—no sweets or anything else to titillate the palate. It was a bit tough on me when I was with him, though, as I was used to diving into a Brahmin restaurant any time my sweet tooth begged for something yummy in the sweet (or savory) department!

As for shelter, Dick could put his head down just about anywhere and get a good night's sleep. Usually, when he was in a village, his hosts took "pity" on him and gave him a standard village cot of knotted rope to sleep on. But, I'm sure he would agree, though they felt they were doing the hospitable thing for him, these cots were not comfortable and were usually much too short for either him or me. (As a result, I usually got a much less restful night on these cots than I could have on the cement floor.) Dick usually slept on a longer fold-away cot at his headquarters, made to order by the local village carpenter.

Dick didn't require much space to live or to carry on his work. One room was usually sufficient. At the Vatalagundu Sarvodaya Ashram, his small building was thatched, like any other village dwelling.

What about his possessions? Frankly, I saw few of these when he lived on the plains, other than his vehicle and a few tools. In Kodai, his possessions amounted to books and a few tools and supplies, some of which may have belonged to the Kodaikanal Ashram Fellowship and were used to help maintain the place. When Dick traveled in India, he always traveled by bus or third-class train. I never knew of his sneaking onto a second-class car, as I sometimes did whenever berths were available in second class but not in third class. Using the cheapest transportation was important to him in identifying with the poor.

When Dick came to the States to visit family and friends, he had to travel like most everybody else, economy class. To this extent, he admitted he was of two worlds—the world of his mission and life and the world of his family.

SOME POSTSCRIPT MEMORIES

Dick would mention on occasion, in a sort of matter-of-fact way, that the biggest failure of his life had been in his marriage and his breaking up with Mildred[21]. He would often say, particularly in his last few years, how much he missed seeing his children more often. He recognized the importance of family. In his last letter to me, March 20, 1984, he began with some thoughts entitled, "Blessed Is the Home." In this, we read:

> The Home is the primary cooperative unit of Society.
> Here is the concentration of the creativity of the Creator.
> Naturally, the Home is blessed, inspired, strengthened if it serves this basic purpose of life.
> The Home should be the center of the Healing Ministry
> The Family should be the heart of the Nurturing Ministry.

In the end, it is clear to me that for Dick, the family that held the most significant part of his heart were those friends and those poor he identified with in India, for he would remember his Master's words, "Here are my mother and my brothers! Whoever does the will of God is my brother, and sister, and mother."

Dick had a vocabulary that was uniquely his. For example, he would talk of people's or groups' having 'potential' and say that this person or that group had 'potential.' You had to know him to understand in what sense he felt the individual or group was demonstrating 'potential.' It meant the potentiality to grow into a position of leadership to inspire others by example,

---

21. Mildred and her older daughter Mearl Marie visited my family and me once while we were living in Davis California 1961–67 after our first term in India. I believe it was in 1964. And on our way to Minnesota in 1966 where I took a summer course in groundwater hydrology, Jane, Skyler, Jeremy and I visited Mildred at the farm in Iowa where she had moved to. She knew we were good friends with Dick, but nevertheless was very friendly to us.

to adopt a life of non-violence and cooperation in all aspects. Also, Dick frequently spoke of people committing or indulging in 'nonsense.' Sometimes, the word meant 'tamash' meaning (in Hindi) light-heartedly making fun; sometimes, he used it to connote something bordering on dishonesty. In the latter case, I guess he used the word 'nonsense' because he didn't feel he was in a position to judge any person by using a stronger word.

It seems to me that in a sense, Dick limited his vocabulary in English on purpose, so that it would help to separate him and his mission from 'the world.' A revolution in community living through cooperation based on the needs of the 'least of these' necessarily had to be accompanied by a vocabulary that served the revolution's needs.

Dick had a good practical grasp of Tamil. But here also his vocabulary was limited, though not intentionally limited perhaps as in the case of his English. Also, he lacked a very authentic-sounding Tamil pronunciation. He could certainly get his ideas across in a meeting, but I wondered whether he might have been more effective if his Tamil had been better. At evening village meetings I attended with him, I was very often unable to pick up the meaning of what was said in Tamil as well as he could. But, I think, on the whole, I had a larger vocabulary and more accurate pronunciation. But probably it didn't matter to his ministry. I wondered whether he might have been laughed at sometimes because of his Tamil pronunciation, at least by some of the people on the periphery of the movement.

Yet the Bible teaches us through St. Paul that "the foolishness of God is wiser than men, and the weakness of God is stronger than men." And from Gandhiji's "Songs from Prison," we read a related verse: "The power of the spirit ruleth all wisdom; one man in whom this power dwelleth will shake a hundred who are only learned." Keithahnji shook many hundreds of us in India—many Indians, and also a few Westerners.

What then was there about Keithahn? What was the source of his power—the power to persuade, inspire, and sometimes bring a sense of guilt? I guess it was his personality combined with his faith. He was, well, relentless and hard-driving, but at the same time, gentle and understanding of human failings because he recognized his own failings. He enjoyed poking gentle fun, but never in a way that would demean the person he was talking about.

I mentioned earlier that Dick, more than almost anyone else I knew, could see quickly through to the core of a moral problem or dilemma. That's because he had his eyes set on the horizon. In my opinion, he never looked for nor acted in any way to obtain the short-lived praises of people, but he kept his eye on the goal. Whatever the moral and just principle was in a given situation, that is what he would keep his sights on. Anything less would amount to a capitulation to what was weak; anything less would mean he had failed his Master.

Most of all, Dick was exciting to be with; he was rarely 'down.' He had hope and had it abundantly, and he believed in you and in every person he met. Dick knew you could take that one additional step that would demonstrate your greater commitment to the needs of your fellows and thus bring the Kingdom of Heaven one step closer. He had *the* missionary spirit, in the sense that he just knew that he was tied to the Way Jesus would have us tread. There was no doubt in his mind, at least he never showed a glimmer of doubt when I was around. That was Dick, and I miss him a lot.

I'll never forget the sound of his voice nor fail to remember his words, such as "We've not yet come up to the mark," which he often said. What was the 'mark'? I think it was caring so much for all God's people that we, in some sense, give up our life, the "good" things of our life, to serve them in humility. Dick set the 'mark' high. I love that man.

Dick's older daughter Mearl Marie became one of our friends. After college, she took her medical training in India and became an MD. In 1967, we visited her when she was serving in a mission hospital in Ambala, Haryana, very close to Punjab state. We were on our way home to New Delhi from making a quick visit to the hill station Simla, in the Himalayan foothills. This was during our second term in India during 1967–71.

After Dick died, I kept in contact with Mearl Marie. She had moved to Minnesota and had recently married a Norwegian bachelor farmer. And when I took Hendrik back to India in 1991 for a visit, I visited a small farm near Vatalagundu at her request. It was a farm of probably 10 acres in size on land owned by the Keithahn Sathya Trust, which Dick had set up years before he died. The farm grew a variety of fruits and vegetables to serve as a demonstration to nearby farmers. Mearl Marie had asked me to act as a go-between with the farmer running the farm and her as a Trust director. I inspected the farm and discussed a few issues with the farmer, including the parcel's property boundaries, and then sent her a report of my findings. The 2019 annual newsletter from the Christian Fellowship Hospital in Oddanchatram noted that the Keithahn Sathya Trust continued to sponsor the Fellowship's elder-age programs and evening tuition centers. Later Mearl Marie sent me some detailed material about her father that I found invaluable in writing this chapter.

NEWBIGIN

Lesslie Newbigin, circa 1975—
courtesy of the *International Bulletin of Missionary Research*

I met Lesslie Newbigin sometime in 1956, soon after we arrived in India for the first time. Unlike the old days, we were not working under the American Madura Mission through the American Board of Commissioners for Foreign Missions (ABCFM), but rather we had been seconded *by* the ABCFM to the Madurai-Ramnad Diocese of the Church of South India (CSI) to do rural development work. Lesslie had been elected to be the Diocese's first Bishop back in 1947, immediately after the CSI itself was founded.

Lesslie was a most charming person, even endearing. He wore his authority as Bishop very comfortably, but he also did an excellent job as a listener. He had the perfect mixture of compassion and faith on the one hand and a commanding presence on the other, very fitting for his role as Bishop of Madurai-Ramnad (1947–59) and later as Bishop of Madras (1965–74) both in the Church of South India (CSI).

He was also simply brilliant as a thinker and writer. As a writer, he was prolific, writing at least 25 books, including his autobiography, *Unfinished Agenda* (Saint Andrew Press, 1993), and numerous papers and reports that served as discussion papers for the many ecumenical conferences and theological study groups he attended over his life. Another edition of his autobiography was published posthumously in 2009 by Wipf and Stock Publishers[1].

Lesslie *was* my boss from the middle of 1956 until sometime in 1959, at which point Bishop George Devadass, a fine Christian leader, took over from him. As a boss, Lesslie gave me a long leash. I could design my own village projects pretty much as I saw fit, in consultation with local Indian church leaders.

I remember Lesslie admonishing me only once as my boss. Word had gotten out after we had moved to Kallimandaiyam that I was working overly hard and sometimes skipping, so it went, the needs of my wife and children. He wrote me a note saying that the Lord did not require my working so hard, to the extent of possibly ignoring my family's needs. In other words, he felt it could be perceived that I was trying to earn my salvation through my work, rather than depending on the grace of God. I wrote him back based on St. Paul's letter to the Philippians 2:12–13: "I'm trying to work out my salvation with fear and trembling; for I believe it is God who is at work in me, enabling me both to will and to work for his good pleasure."

Lesslie would usually set a demanding schedule for *himself*, whether it was visiting village congregations, meetings with diocesan officials in Madurai, writing books, or traveling to Europe for high-level meetings connected with the World Council of Churches (WCC) or the International Missionary Council (IMC).

As mentioned earlier, Lesslie was responsible for seeking out Raja Rao and convincing him that he should be my Tamil teacher. That was a great

---

1. Newbigin, *Unfinished Agenda*.

gift to me personally, for Raja Rao was my eyes and ears into the Indian society and the Indian church.

Also, as mentioned in the previous chapter, there were the alternating and usually opposing articles in the *South Indian Churchman* and the *Guardian* by Dick Keithahn and Lesslie. In his *Unfinished Agenda*, Lesslie lamented that Dick had no objection to participating in the Gandhian practice of common (inter-faith) worship. He said that his (Lesslie's) Indian colleagues were solidly with him in rejecting the practice. This was the only place in his autobiography that mentions Keithahn. He made no mention of Dick's remarkable Christian impact on Indian youth.

Lesslie's sense of urgency concerning unity among the Christian denominations was prompted by his experience as a young missionary during his first assignment at age 30 when he and his wife arrived in Kanchipuram in Tamil Nadu. He came there as a missionary under the Church of Scotland. Lesslie took quickly to the Tamil language and began his work as a village evangelist. He became troubled by the competing denominational missions that often resulted in a separation of converts by caste. He saw this as a public contradiction to the gospel of reconciliation and a primary obstacle to missionary work.

According to his autobiography, it was in Kanchipuram where he experienced and began to appreciate Christian leaders' exchanging theological concepts with spiritual leaders of Hinduism. And, as he wrote, he "became more and more sure that the 'point of contact' for the Gospel is rather in the ordinary secular experiences of human life than in the sphere of religion." He was beginning to see that religion could be a way of protecting oneself from reality.

Lesslie had an appreciation and affection for M. M. Thomas, the highly-regarded Indian Christian theologian and one of the architects, along with Lesslie, of the modern ecumenical movement. Thomas also expertly articulated the need for Christians to be in community with non-Christians. Lesslie had assisted in the inauguration of the Christian Institute for the Study of Religion and Society in Bangalore. M. M. Thomas was associated with it ever since its inception in 1955. Lesslie and Thomas were also connected through their mutual participation in the World Council of Churches and their joint efforts to promote discussions of conversion vs. community in the Indian church.

During 1941–42, Thomas was in Bangalore, where he became a student of Dick Keithahn at the Social Workers' Brotherhood. There, reading voraciously, he undertook an in-depth self-study of Christianity, Marxism, Gandhism, nationalism, and Christian social thought.

During that time, it appears Thomas came down on the side of both Marxism and allegiance to Christ. At one point during 1941, at age 25, he decided to apply for ordination in the church *and* for membership in the Communist party at the same time! He was refused on both counts! As he relates[2]:

> the church committee did not think my ethics were very good when I was asked to tell them about my attitude to violence because I had grown Marxian in my understanding. I said there were occasions when violence would be necessary. That was the time the Gandhian ethics were popular. Then, of course the Communist Party wouldn't admit me because I was too Christian, and I said 'wherever I am, I will do evangelistic work,' and they thought I would be a disturbance to the party. So that's how I was refused.

During the late 1960s and early 1970s, Lesslie and Thomas began a dialogue in print, a debate as it were with each other, over the role of accepting community versus conversion of non-Christians. Among other things, Thomas called for a new definition of the substance of what it is to acknowledge Christ Jesus as Lord and Savior. He wanted Lesslie to acknowledge 'Christian' faith as being present in many who cannot or do not acknowledge Jesus in how the church has historically acknowledged him. But Leslie responded that an acceptance of Jesus Christ as we know him in the Bible, as the absolute Lord of all things, must be part of the Christian faith's minimal expression. He said the acceptance of Jesus Christ creates a kind of solidarity among those who have this acceptance in common, which leads to meeting together as a fellowship to celebrate with words, songs, and formal actions. Lesslie's debate with M. M. Thomas never led to a satisfactory conclusion or understanding, but it provided an issue for discussion by younger theologians.

Lesslie was a firm believer in the so-called 'mass conversions' that had occurred in the Palani-Oddanchatram-Kallimandaiyam area, a few years before our moving to Kallimandaiyam in 1958. Because of the impressive number of mass conversions, they began to be known collectively as the 'South India Miracle' by Christian evangelists. Rev. Thangaiya handled the Oddanchatram pastorate during most of those years, to be followed, close to the time when we arrived in the area, by Rev. Packianathan. The mass conversions involved all the members of a single caste in a given village confessing that Jesus was their Lord. In most cases, the caste involved was one of two Dalit groups in the area. It was a subject of either considerable

---

2. Tisdale, Leonora Tubbs. "The formation of a prophet of the cross." In Athyal et al., *The Life, Legacy and Theology of M. M. Thomas*, 35–37.

enthusiasm or worried concern among educated Christians in South India. Their feelings depended on whether they believed the conversions were from the heart or whether the conversions were based on hopes that they, the converts, would have access to more education, possible loans, or even better access to health care at Christian clinics and hospitals.

I myself did not know the inner hearts of the people in my area who had converted recently. I believe it's safe to say that in most cases, there was hope among the converts that they would receive some help to lift them up socially and economically. I'm also sure some individual members converted because they believed that their spiritual salvation was through Jesus. Most of those converted realized that by becoming Christians, their sense of self-worth had been raised up, if not their social standing. I know that in my service projects, I made it clear that I helped all the Dalits of a village, whether they were Hindu or Christian. (There were few to no Muslims in my village area.)

The mass conversions of Dalit groups were generally not welcomed by the Hindu caste people of the area. Some of them viewed the conversions as 'forced' conversions, with the Indian and foreign missionaries' using promises of pecuniary aid. Some of them saw that by these poor Dalits' converting to Christianity, they, the Hindu farmers, might lose power over them, for each of the male Dalits in a village was attached to one of the Hindu farmers. They worked for the farmers in the fields and also were pretty much at their beck and call at other times.

The politicians were also aware of this and would often complain about what Christian leaders were doing to effect mass conversions in their districts. As mentioned earlier, in December 1959, the local member of the Madras State Legislative Assembly complained about me in a Tamil-language newspaper. He said that my distributing U.S. surplus milk powder was simply an effort to convert Dalits. Fortunately, I had two Hindu friends in the taluk (township) office who defended me. In response to the rains failing, it was simply an act of compassion rather than proselytization. I made it clear that I was distributing the milk powder and U.S. surplus grains in a completely unbiased manner.

Lesslie felt it important for people to know about the books he had published and how many theological papers he had written. He wanted folks to know how many high-level theologians he was, or had been, in conversation with, as described in his autobiography *Unfinished Agenda*. Lesslie as my boss and my bishop paid one or two visits to us in Kallimandaiyam. On one occasion, he and one of his colleagues were having lunch with us in our home when a person of some note came up in the conversation. Lesslie was at pains to inform us that he knew and had worked with that person.

As he evolved as a Christian, Lesslie began to believe in the importance of Christians' taking stands and taking part in actions on peace and justice issues. At one point in his early years, he became a pacifist and then later reneged on that belief as Hitler's war-like actions became more ominous. Lesslie insisted all peace and justice causes must be subservient to, and motivated by, faith in Christ. He abhorred any Christian's performing good works for secular reasons. He believed very strongly that faith in the God of Jesus should be the source for all good works.

Lesslie was keen on the church doing whatever it could to strengthen the village economy by building on local skills as much as possible. But he balked at too much foreign money coming in, such that a dependent mentality could develop in the villagers. He felt the better approach was to evoke a commitment in the village people themselves and then offer something like seed money commensurate with the project's scale that they themselves would propose.

Lesslie not only talked the talk but also walked the walk. He joined with other church leaders to physically help the victims in villages affected by major floods in South India and victims of significant inter-caste violence in village areas.

There was a terrible cyclone in southern Tamil Nadu in December 1955 when over 160 of the CSI's village churches, schools, and parsonages were destroyed in a single night. When Lesslie learned that relief supplies were not reaching the affected villages, he took a party of volunteer relief workers down the coast to transfer a load of grain from a train to a boat. But when the boat engines failed, they spent most of the night tossing helplessly in the Bay of Bengal waters. Ultimately they got the grain to the village area where it was needed. Then government officials gave Lesslie's group the responsibility of supplying food to 200 villages in that area.

One day in September 1957, diocesan officials received news that a group of 600 Maravars, the dominant landowning caste, had taken up arms against the Christian Dalit group in Veerambal village in Ramnad District. Lesslie and other officials from the Diocese rushed to the village by car. They spent the following days comforting the bereaved, tending to the wounded, and visiting Maravar villages to try to bring about peace. As mentioned in the previous chapter, Keithahn and his group did much the same in those difficult days in Ramnad district.

Their Christian faith had given the Dalit group in Veerambal a sense of pride that they didn't have before their conversion, bolstered by their superior education. The Maravars felt that the Dalit group was acting too uppity for their liking. The attacks took place while the Christians were gathered in the local church, and large numbers of the Christians were either killed or badly injured.

In his autobiography, *Unfinished Agenda*, Lesslie recounts his visit when Vinoba Bhave[3] was in his Diocese. In 1958 or thereabouts, Lesslie spent a day following Vinoba on one of his long, patient walks on foot from village to village. Lesslie remembered that he listened to Vinoba preach "a superb sermon" on a text from Romans 12. Though Lesslie said he was captivated by Vinoba's beautiful spirit, he remained unconvinced at the end of a long personal discussion with him, in which Lesslie said that Vinoba didn't effectively answer his questions. Lesslie concluded, "The long experience of missions had shown the futility of giving land to people who had no capital to invest in it, no resources against bad seasons, and no hereditary experience as landowners."

When we were in Kallimandaiyam, Rev. Pakianathan, our pastor, one day reflected on Lesslie's stint as his bishop. He remembered a day when he and Lesslie were making the rounds of Packianathan's congregations in the Oddanchatram-Kallimandaiyam area. (Rev. Packianathan was pastor to 55 village congregations in that area!) It was a particularly hot day, and Lesslie was bearing up magnificently, preaching and greeting congregants happily while sweat was dripping noticeably all over his face. He stood up to it, seemingly without any stress. When Rev. Packianathan told me the story, he conveyed how much he admired Lesslie for this, despite the Bishop's being a foreigner and living at a far higher lifestyle than Packianathan and his family. Rev. Packianathan had ambivalent feelings about me as a foreign missionary in his country. But I doubt that my higher salary was adequately balanced in his mind by the kind of suffering and persistence that Lesslie commonly displayed.

When my family and I returned to Tamil Nadu in 1968 to live in the city of Madras (now Chennai) under Action for Food Production (AFPRO), we were happy to learn that Lesslie had become the CSI Bishop of the Madras Diocese, a position he held from 1965 to 1974. He encountered many challenges in that position, as he described in his autobiography. I did not see him very frequently during our time there (1968–71). I remember my attending one of his Bible studies in a church close to our home. We talked afterward, and he commended me for my work in AFPRO.

Four of Lesslie's most important books are believed to be *The Household of God* (1953), *The Open Secret: Sketches for a Missionary Theology*

---

3. Leader of the land-gift (*Bhoodan*) movement and disciple of Gandhi.

(1978), *Foolishness to the Greeks: The Gospel and Western Culture* (1986), and *The Gospel in a Pluralist Society* (1989). Some of his influential books, such as *South India Diary* (1951), *The Reunion of the Church* (1948), *The Household of God* (1953), and *Sin and Salvation* (1956), were translated *from* his original Tamil! He even wrote a book, *Christian Freedom in the Modern World*, when he and his wife Helen were on board the ship taking them to India for the first time! And thirty years later, he learned that that book had played some part in the early development of the theological thinking of M. M. Thomas.

After his retirement in the U.K. in 1975, he tried to communicate the serious need for the church to once again take the Gospel to post-Christian Western culture, which he viewed not as a secular society without gods but as a pagan society with false gods. His most significant contribution to the church, I believe, is in his efforts to promote both unity among the many church denominations in Christendom and the missionary call to bring Christ to non-believers.

Many theologians have studied and written on Lesslie's thinking and theology, for example, in 2018, Michael Gaheen published his book entitled *The Church and its Vocations: Lesslie Newbigin's Missionary Ecclesiology*. Theologian and Lesslie Newbigin historian Geoffrey Wainwright has stated that when the 20th-century church's history is written, Lesslie Newbigin should be considered one of the top ten or twelve most influential Christian thinkers. Lesslie died at age 88 at his home in Birmingham, England, in January 1998. I admired that man deeply.

GLOSSARY

ABCFM	See 'American Board of Commissioners for Foreign Missions.'
Action for Food Production (AFPRO)	Voluntary development agency in India started in 1967 funded in large part by Western relief agencies
AFPRO	I worked for them 1967–71, being seconded to them by the UCBWM
Allahabad	City in North India located on the Ganges River in Uttar Pradesh state
Alvars	Tamil Vaishnavite saints/poets who wrote hymns in praise of Vishnu and his avatars, 7th to 10th century AD
Ambilikai	Village on the road between Kallimandaiyam and Oddanchatram
American Board of Commissioners for Foreign Missions (ABCFM)	Mission board of the Congregational churches that sent the Mills family to South India in 1956
American College	College in Madurai, Tamil Nadu, started in 1881 by missionaries of the American Madura Mission
American Madura Mission (AMM)	American mission group located in Madurai District of Tamil Nadu supported by the ABCFM
amma	'mother' or 'lady' in Tamil
Andersonpatti	Small hamlet on the road between Oddanchatram and Vatalagundu
Andhra Pradesh	Southern state in India located immediately north of Tamil Nadu
Anglo-Indians	Offspring of mixed marriages/unions between usually British men and Indian women.

167

GLOSSARY

Aruppukkotai	Indian city in Madurai District about 30 miles due south of the city of Madurai
ashram (Hindu)	Place for spiritual meditation and renewal; *or*, a stage of life of a Hindu caste male
ayah	'nursemaid' in Tamil
ayya	'sir' or 'gentleman' in Tamil
bajan	'songs of devotion to God'
Balwadi	Nursery school
Bangalore	City in the southern Indian state of Karnataka. Its modern name is *'Bengaluru.'*
Basic Education	Type of village education that Gandhi espoused which was adopted by the Indian government soon after Independence
Basic elementary schools	Schools in India that were founded on the principles of 'Basic Education.'
Baskeran	R. Trinity Baskeran who worked with me in the Kallimandaiyam area 1968–69 and later served as Bishop of the CSI Diocese of Vellore
Bharata Natyam	Classical South Indian dance
Bhogpur	Small city near the Himalayas in the state of Punjab, India
Bhoodan	Land-gift movement started by Gandhi's disciple Vinoba Bhave in the 1950s
Bishop Devadass	Bishop of the Diocese of Madurai-Ramnad from 1959 to 1978
Boduvarpatti	Village in the vicinity of Oddanchatram and Chatrapatti
Brahma	god the creator - one of the three principal deities in the Hindu pantheon
Brahmin	A caste in Indian society usually believed to be the highest caste
Bullocks	oxen
Bund	An embankment; a linear mound separating agricultural fields in India
Calcutta	Major city in eastern India, now called 'Kolkata.'
Cantonment	Military garrison or station in British India found in the larger cities of India
Cape Comorin	Southernmost town in India. Known now as *'Kanyakumari.'*
Carnatic music	Classical music of South India, usually performed by a small ensemble of musicians and vocalist

GLOSSARY

Carol Weeber	American missionary to India. She worked near me and was headquartered then in Chatrapatti
Caste system	Artificial construct which sets the presumed supremacy of one group of people against the supposed inferiority of other groups on the basis of ancestry
Chakliar	Former designation of the leather-worker Dalit caste
Chandra	Daughter of our nursemaid and cook Pappu
Chatrapatti	Small village between Oddanchatram and Palani; headquarters for Carol Weeber
Chennai	Capital city of the state of Tamil Nadu (Madras), located on the Bay of Bengal
Chettiyar	A "forward" caste often associated with being in the mercantile business
Chinniah	A particular Christian family in Madurai known to Raja Rao
cholam	'sorghum' in Tamil
Christian Dalit	A Dalit Christian
Christian Fellowship Hospital (CFH)	Located in Oddanchatram, South India; administered by a Christian fellowship group originating from Kerala
Christian Medical Fellowship	Located in Oddanchatram, South India; a Christian fellowship group originating from Kerala
Church of South India (CSI)	A united Christian church in South India, formed from several protestant denominations in 1947
Church World Service	Protestant relief agency associated with the National Council of Churches of the U.S.
Coaker's Walk	A walk in Kodaikanal providing an astounding view of the plains 6,000 feet below
Collector	Government administrator of a District, comparable to a county in the U.S.
Conductor	Ticket collector on a public bus in South India
Congress Party	Political party started by Gandhi which was responsible for India obtaining its independence
Cumbum Valley	A north-south oriented valley on the eastern side of the western ghats in Madurai District
Dalits	A caste grouping that formerly was considered the lowest class of the society, the "Untouchables."
Damaris	Andrew and Jane's adopted daughter
Dapsone	Drug formerly used singly to stop the advance of leprosy in leprosy patients

GLOSSARY

Deenabandhu-puram	Village created by a pastor (Rev. Joseph John) in the Vellore area of Tamil Nadu
Devakottai	A city located in Ramnad District
Dharapuram	A city in Tirupur District in Tamil Nadu, about 16 miles north of Kallimandaiyam
dhoti	Garment worn by men in India that covers the body from the waist to the ankles
Dindigul	City then in the northwest part of Madurai District; Now it is the headquarters of the new Dindigul District
Doble	Name of a British Methodist missionary couple assigned to the Kurur District north of what is now the Dindigul District.
dorai	'A respected man' in Tamil
doraisani	'A respected woman' in Tamil; often explicitly applied to missionary women in India
Dravidian	Pertaining to the South Indian culture. Dravidian people are believed to have originally populated the Indus-Valley civilizations circa 3000 BC.
Dravidian languages	Major South Indian languages: Tamil, Telugu, Kannada, and Malayalam
Gallups	David and Padma Gallup, missionaries to the CSI, Madurai-Ramnad Diocese under the UCBWM beginning in 1959
Gandhian workers	People who volunteer to work to fulfill Gandhi's goal of Sarvodaya and Satyagraha
Gandhigram	Institution near Dindigul offering a variety of training, all related to improving the lives of villagers
Gounder	A "forward" caste often associated with landowners practicing farming in Tamil Nadu
Gramdan	A village in which the majority of landowners have given one-sixth of their land for the use of the landless people in their village
Guinea worm	A disease common in South Indian villages caused by drinking water polluted with larvae of an organism that becomes a worm that exits the legs painfully
Harappa	One of the cities of the Indus-Valley civilizations
Helen	Andrew's wife since December 1996
Hendrik	Oldest son of Andrew and Jane Mills
Indo-Aryans	Indo-Aryan people believed to have migrated into India starting in 1800 BC from present-day Kazakhstan, Uzbekistan, and Turkmenistan

Indo-European language group	A broad linguistic group that includes most European languages as well as Sanskrit and modern North Indian languages derived from Sanskrit
Indus River civilization	Early urban civilization located in the Indus River valley circa 3000 BC, in present-day Pakistan
Iyengar	A sub-class of the Brahmin caste consisting of Vaishnavites, worshippers of Vishnu and his avatars Krishna and Rama
Iyer	A sub-class of the Brahmin caste consisting of Shaivites, worshippers of Shiva
Jaganathan, S.	A disciple of Vinoba Bhave and former leader of the *Bhoodan* and Sarvodaya movement in Tamil Nadu
Jaggery	A dark sugar or syrup derived from the palmyra palm tree found in abundance in Ramnad
Jane	Andrew's ex-wife married 1952–1992
Jayaprakash Narayan	Graduate of UC Berkeley and Indian independence activist and socialist; later devoted himself solely to the Sarvodaya movement
Jeevanasen	Tamil instructor in the language school in Bangalore, brother of Jothimuthu, our first Tamil teacher.
Jeremy	Youngest son of Andrew and Jane Mills
jibba	Shirt for men used throughout India
Joseph John	A pastor in Vellore District of Tamil Nadu who formed a village which he named Deenabandhupuram, based on Gandhian principles
Jothimuthu	Professor of Tamil in American College who gave us our first Tamil classes
Kālakshepam	Presentation of stories of Hindu saints or gods, or stories about Jesus, in song.
Kallar	A "forward" caste often believed to be 'night-time robbers' but are commonly landowning farmers.
Kallimandaiyam	'Our village' during 1958–1961, nine miles north of Oddanchatram
Kanchipuram	City located about 45 miles west of Chennai; it's known as the 'Temple City.'
Kannada	Dravidian language spoken in the southern state of Karnataka
Kannivadi	Small city between Oddanchatram and Vatalagundu
Karnam	Village accountant in Tamil Nadu, often considered the headman of a village
Karnataka	Southern state in India. The major city is Bangalore (*Bengaluru*).

GLOSSARY

Katpadi	Small city near Vellore about 85 miles west of Chennai
kavadi	Burden carried by a devotee to the Murugan temple in Palani in exchange for a favor to be bestowed on the devotee
kavalai	System of irrigation in which a pair of bullocks is driven down a slope to bring water up from a well to fill an irrigation channel
Keeranur	Small village northeast of Kallimandaiyam
Keithahn	R. Richard Keithahn was a Christian missionary who served in India from 1925 until his death in 1984, with two forcible departures to the U.S. due to his association with the Gandhian Independence movement.
Keithahn Sathya Trust	Trust fund set up by Keithahn to fund medical, educational, and agricultural development projects in Tamil Nadu
Kellys	Christian missionaries to the American College in Madurai supported by the UCBWM starting in 1960
Kerala	Southern state in India, just west of Tamil Nadu. Capital city is *Thiruvananthapuram*
khadi	Cloth made of hand-spun thread, worn by workers in the independence movement as popularized by Gandhi.
Kodai Ashram Fellowship	Fellowship supporting and maintaining the Kodaikanal Ashram
Kodai International School	American school in Kodai set up for children of American missionaries. Later evolved into an international school.
Kodaikanal ('Kodai')	Small city in the 'Palani Hills' (Western Ghats), developed by missionaries from Europe and America to create a cool place to vacation
Kondarangimalai	Conical-shaped hill three miles east of our village
Krishnammal	Wife of S. Jaganathan, *Gramdan* and Sarvodaya leader in Tamil Nadu
kudi	'To drink' in Tamil
kumbu	A type of nutritious and delicious millet, one of the staples of village people in Tamil Nadu
Kunjamma	Name of the nurse in the Christian Fellowship who was the first one to move to Oddanchatram a few days before Dr. Tharien and his family came to start the hospital
Lorry	British English for 'truck.'
M. M. Thomas	Well-regarded Christian theologian hailing from Kerala; major participant in the worldwide ecumenical movement; also an excellent articulator of Indian Christian nationalism
Madras	Capital city of the state of Tamil Nadu, now known as *Chennai*

GLOSSARY

Madura	British spelling of *Madurai*, district headquarters for Madurai District
Madura Mission	same as American Madura Mission (AMM)
Madurai District	Political entity located in the southern part of Tamil Nadu. One of 38 districts in the state.
Madurai-Ramnad Diocese	A diocese of the CSI, which initially included only the political districts of Madurai and Ramnad.
Maharashtra	State in the west-central part of India. Bombay (now *'Mumbai'*) is the capital of the state.
Malayalam	One of four major Dravidian languages. It is spoken in the state of Kerala
Malayali	Refers to people living in Kerala or those who speak Malayalam
Mandavadi	A small village two miles south of Kallimandaiyam
Mangalados	Name of a young Christian Dalit man living in the village of Navakani
manvatti	short-handled mattock
Maravar	A "forward" caste often believed to be 'day-time robbers.' Maravars are also landowning farmers in Ramnad District
Mariamma	Wife of Dr. A. K. Tharien, a founding member of the Christian Medical Fellowship in Oddanchatram
Mass conversions	Conversion of entire caste group in a village from Hinduism to Christianity
Mearl Marie	Older daughter of Dick and Mildred Keithahn
Mildred McKie	Dick Keithahn's ex-wife; She took her maiden name after their divorce in the 1960s.
Miraj Medical College	The medical college in Maharashtra where Dr. Tharien took his medical training and was part of, and helped form, a Christian Fellowship there
Missionary Union	Organization in Kodaikanal to foster social events among missionaries
Mohenjo-Daro	One of the cities of the Indus-Valley civilizations
Munnar	A town in the state of Kerala in the western ghats, famous for tea plantations
munshi	Teacher
munsif	Headman of a village
Murugan	Hindu god worshipped in his temple in Palani, then on the western edge of Madurai District

Murugaswami	Name of a Gounder friend of mine in Navakani
Muslim	Religious adherent to Islam and the prophet Muhammad. This is the proper spelling, which when sounded out leads to the correct pronunciation of the term ('mooslim')
Mysore	(*Mysuru*), city in the southern side of Karnataka state. It was the capital of the Kingdom of Mysore from 1399 to 1947.
Naicker	A mid-level caste, members of which are mostly devoted to farming.
Naomi	A midwife and nurse practitioner who was assigned to the small clinic in Mandavadi, 2 miles south of Kallimandaiyam
Navakani	Village where I took the contract to construct a new drinking-water well for the Dalit population
Newbigin	Lesslie Newbigin was bishop of the Diocese of Madurai-Ramnad from 1947 to 1959
Nirmala	Only daughter of Dr. Tharien and his wife Mariamma
Oddanchatram	Small town located equidistant from Dindigul and Palani, 18 miles. Then located on the western side of Madurai District
Oddanchatram Fellowship Hospital	Hospital established and administered by the Christian Fellowship in the town of Oddanchatram since 1955
Packiammal	Bible woman who was stationed in the village of Veriapoor by the Madurai-Ramnad Diocese of the CSI
Paddy fields	Rice fields
Palani	City on the far western side of the then Madurai District. The British termed it 'Palni.' Home of the famous Murugan temple.
Palani Hills	The section of the Western Ghats bordering the then Madurai District. The British called them the 'Palni Hills.'
Palmyra palm trees	Type of palm tree common in Ramnad and south; yields both jaggery and toddy, an alcoholic drink.
pandal	A shelter of upright poles supporting a roof that is usually of palm-leaf matting
Pappu	Nickname of our loyal Ayah and cook. Her full name was *Annapurani*, 'the fullness of food.'
Paraiyar	A former designation for the musician Dalit caste
Pasumalai	A southwestern suburb to the city of Madurai
pavam	'Sin' in Tamil
Periyar dam	The dam in the Western Ghats that provides water to the River Vaigai, at the banks of which stands the city of Madurai.
Petrol bunk	gasoline station

GLOSSARY

Petromax	A pressurized kerosene lantern giving bright light
Pillai	Last (caste) name of a person belonging to the Velalar caste
Ponnusami	Rev. Ponnusami was the pastor of the Vatalagundu CSI church when we were there.
Pooja	Act of worship to a Hindu deity
Poruloor	A large village about six miles west of Kallimandaiyam
Public Law 480 (P.L. 480)	The U.S. public law that provided for the donation of U.S. surplus foodstuffs to countries suffering from famine
puramboke	Tamil for government land or lands held in common
puttu	Grains, such as ragi, prepared for meals by steaming
Radha	Hindu goddess of love, tenderness, compassion, and devotion
ragi	A type of millet, used by village people as one of their staples
Raja Rao	Our beloved Tamil teacher
Rajagopalachari, C.	Governor-General of India 1948–1950 and Chief Minister of Madras state 1952–1954
Ramachandram, Dr. G.	Husband of T. S. Soundram who worked together to create Gandhigram and the nearby Kasturba Hospital
Ramanathapuram	City on the coast of the Bay of Bengal and the District capital of Ramnad
Ramesh	K. Ramesh is a friend of ours in Madurai. He runs the Southern Roadways division of the TVS Group, which was started by his grandfather
Ramnad	Generally pertaining to Ramnad District, the boundaries of which have been redrawn since we were there
Ranchanyapuram	Christian (CSI) institution consisting of a school and training center for girls, close to K. Puthur 3 miles north of Madurai
Rev. Baninga	CSI Presbyter who ran for Bishop of Madurai-Ramnad Diocese, but failed in a CSI Synod vote in May of 2013
Rev. Devapragasam	CSI Presbyter who served as Local Council chairman at Dindigul and later Thirumangalam under the Madurai-Ramnad Diocese.
Rev. Joseph	CSI Presbyter who ran for Bishop of Madurai-Ramnad Diocese, and succeeded in a CSI Synod vote in May of 2013
Rev. Packianathan	CSI Presbyter for the Oddanchatram pastorate with 55 congregations when we were there.
Rev. Thangaiya	CSI Presbyter at Oddanchatram about 1953–1957
Rev. Thangaiyah	CSI Presbyter at Kallimandaiyam about 2010–?

GLOSSARY

Rev. Williams	CSI Presbyter who served as Local Council Chairman for the Dindigul local council during the approximate period 1958–61
Riggs	Ed and Fran Riggs were medical missionaries to the Madurai-Ramnad Diocese of the CSI through the UCBWM
Roorkee	A city in the foothills of the Himalayas, Uttar Pradesh, India
Russell Chandran	Principal of the United Theological College in Bangalore at least during the 1950s
Ruth Seabury	A member of the ABCFM, who visited the Keithahn family in Bangalore in the late 1930s
Sabarmathi Ashram	Gandhi's ashram in Ahmedabad, Gujarat: He termed it as 'Harijan Ashram,' which was his headquarters during 1917–1930.
Sam	Keithahn's secretary and driver during the 1980s until Keithahn's death in 1984
Samsudeen	A Muslim building contractor living in Oddanchatram at least during the 1950s and 1960s
Samuel	The name of two lay catechists: one stationed in Kallimandaiyam and the other living in Andersonpatti
Sanskrit	The primary ancient Indo-European language from which all the major north Indian languages were derived
sa*ppidu*	'To eat' in Tamil
Sargunam	Name of one of the young men I knew in Navakani 1959–61
Sarvodaya Ashram	An ashram set up by Dick Keithahn in the Vatalagundu area to service the *Bhoodan* and *Gramdan* villages in the area
Sarvodaya Mandal	A Tamil Nadu organization working for Gandhian values and directing the Sarvodaya movement.
Sarvodaya movement	The all-India movement that works for 'the welfare of all,' exemplified by *Bhoodan* and *Gramdan* villages
Shaivite	A worshiper of the god Shiva in all his appearances
Sherwood Eddy	A missionary to South India 1900–1911 under YMCA and ABCFM; His mother Margaret Eddy started Kodaikanal School in 1901 when she was visiting him
Shiva	god the destroyer - one of the three principal deities in the Hindu pantheon
Skyler	Middle son of Andrew and Jane Mills
Sokkiah	J. E. Sokkiah had several administrative posts in the American Madura Mission and more recently in the Diocese of Madurai-Ramnad
South India	The portion of India that presently includes the states of Tamil Nadu, Kerala, Andhra Pradesh, Karnataka, and Telangana

GLOSSARY

South India Churchman	Magazine of the Church of South India
Southern Roadways	Division of the TVS Group that provides public bus service and truck transport of goods services in South India
SPG	Society for the Propagation of the Gospel, the missionary society of the high-church side of the Church of England
Stanley Medical College	Located in Chennai, it is one of the premier medical colleges in Tamil Nadu
Sunyasi	A Hindu ascetic who has renounced the world by abandoning all claims to social or family standing
Susheel, T.	The elder son of A. K. Tharien and Mariamma, who is now on the senior staff of the Oddanchatram Christian Fellowship Hospital
T. S. Krishna	The father of K. Ramesh and one of five sons of the founder of the TVS Group, T. V. Sundram Iyengar
T. S. Soundram	One of three sisters of T. S. Krishna. She worked with Gandhi to achieve independence for India
Tahsildar	The administrative head of the Taluk, which is similar to a township
tali	Marriage necklace, which a Hindu bride puts on during the wedding ceremony
Taluk	A political entity within a District. Several taluks make up a district
Tamarind trees	A leguminous tree found in South India that produces pods, the contents of which are used in cooking
tamash	Light-hearted fun and antics
Tamil	One of four major Dravidian languages; it is spoken in the state of Tamil Nadu and the northern part of Sri Lanka.
Tamil Nadu	A state in South India; one of 28 states in India
Tamil Sangam	Academies of poets and scholars centered in the city of Madurai during the period from approximately the sixth century BC to the third century AD.
Tamilian	One whose mother tongue is Tamil
Tank	A reservoir consisting of collected rainwater behind an earthen dam, often used for irrigation
Telfer Mook	UCBWM Secretary for Southern Asia during 1958–1983
Telugu	One of four major Dravidian languages; spoken primarily in the state of Andhra Pradesh

GLOSSARY

Thanjavur	Thanjavur is a district and the main city in that district—one of the 38 districts of the state of Tamil Nadu. This district is located in the delta of the Cauvery River
Tharien	Dr. A. K. Tharien, a medical doctor who was one of the founders of the Oddanchatram Christian Fellowship Hospital
thenai	One of the nutritious and delicious millets, one of the staples of village people in Tamil Nadu
Thiruvalluvar	Poet who wrote the classical Tamil poem *Tirukkural* about 300 BC
Tiffin	Sort of equivalent to the British afternoon tea. In South India, it usually consists of a sweet followed by a savory dish and coffee
Tirukkural	The classical long Tamil poem written by Thiruvalluvar
Tirunelveli	Tirunelveli is a district and the main city in that district. Immediately south of Madurai District, it is one of 38 districts of the state of Tamil Nadu.
Toddy	An alcoholic drink derived from the juice that comes from the flower shoots of the palmyra tree in South India
Training school	A teachers training institution
TVS group	The current business group in South India that controls all the offshoots of the company started by T. V. Sundram Iyengar in 1911
tyar satham	Rice mixed with curds (unsweetened yogurt)
UCC	United Church Christ, formed in 1957 by the union of Congregational churches and the Evangelical and Reformed Church
Vadivel	Son of Pappu (Annapurani)
Vaigai River	The river that flows (when it flows) through the city of Madurai
Vairanapillai, Sam and Suganthi	Friends of Dick Keithahn living in Madurai. Theirs was a mixed-caste marriage.
Vaishnavite	Worshipper of the god Vishnu and his avatars Krishna and Rama
Valasai	A small village north of Madurai where the Diocese had purchased 2.5 acres of good rice land for Dalits to cultivate
Vatalagundu	A town about 30 miles west of Madurai where the Mills family lived from January 1957 to October 1958, called by the British 'Batlagundu.'
Velalar	A so-called "forward" caste of South India

GLOSSARY

Vellore	A city in Tamil Nadu situated about 86 miles west of Chennai
Velusami Naidu	The name of the headman in the village of Veriapoor, near Oddanchatram
Venkatasami	The name of the headmaster of the CSI Teachers Training school in Vatalagundu
Veriapoor	A village located about three miles from Oddanchatram, where I helped to set up a model tannery
Vinoba Bhave	The disciple of Gandhi who started the *Bhoodan* (land-gift) movement
Vishnu	god the preserver - one of the three principal deities in the Hindu pantheon
Water Buffalo	A common type of bovine livestock in Tamil Nadu, raised for its milk which is extra creamy
Water diviner	Any person who is believed to have the ability to sense strong flows of underground water to choose a site to drill water wells
Wayne University	University in Detroit, Michigan. Now known as 'Wayne State University.'
Western Ghats	Mountain range that reaches an altitude of over 7,000 feet and extends on the western side of India from near Cape Comorin to as far north as Gujarat north of Bombay
Yesudas	A typical Christian name in Tamil Nadu meaning 'servant of Jesus.'

Bibliography

Athyal, Jesudas, George Zachariah, and Monica Melanchthon, eds. *The Life, Legacy and Theology of M. M. Thomas: Only Participants Earn the Right to be Prophets.* New York: Routledge, 2016.

Keithahn, Ralph Richard. *Pilgrimage in India: An Autobiographical Fragment.* Madras: Christian Literature Society, 1973, for the Christian Institute for the Study of Religion & Society, Bangalore.

Laing, Mark. "The International Impact of the Formation of the Church of South India: Bishop Newbigin Versus the Anglican Fathers." *International Bulletin of Missionary Research* 33 (2009) 18–24.

Newbigin, Lesslie. *Unfinished Agenda: An Updated Autobiography.* Eugene, OR: Wipf & Stock, 2009.

Nutt, Rick L. *The Whole Gospel for the Whole World: Sherwood Eddy and the American Protestant Mission.* Macon, GA: Mercer University Press, 1997.

Weeber, Carol. *In Lifting Get Under: A Missionary Nurse's 47 Years in India during India's First Years as a Democracy 1947–1994.* Madras, India: Sabari, 1994.

White, Emmons E. *The Wisdom of the Tamil People.* New Delhi: Munshiram Manoharlal, 1975.

www.ingramcontent.com/pod-product-compliance
Lightning Source LLC
Chambersburg PA
CBHW051925160426
43198CB00012B/2047